CHRISTMAS
~ AT HOME ~

CHRISTMAS
~ AT HOME ~

Gifts, recipes and
decorations for
the holidays

THUNDER BAY
P·R·E·S·S

First published in the United States by
Thunder Bay Press
5880 Oberlin Drive, Suite 400
San Diego, CA 92121-9653
1-800-284-3580
http://www.advmkt.com

Library of Congress Cataloging-in-Publication Data
Amos, Sharon. 1956-
Christmas at home : gifts, recipes, and decorations for the holidays / Sharon Amos
p.   cm.
Includes index.
ISBN 1-57145-167-6
1. Christmas decorations. 2. Handicraft. 3. Christmas cookery.
I. Title.
TT900.C4A47 1998
742.594' 12–dc21   98-28323
CIP

1 2 3 4 5 98 99 00 01 02

Designer: William Mason
Editor: Sharon Amos
Photography and credits: see page 160

Reproduction by Reed Digital

Printed in Hong Kong by Bookbuilders Ltd

CONTENTS

INTRODUCTION

PREPARING FOR *Christmas at home instead of shopping in crowded stores, is infinitely more relaxing and satisfying. Here we've covered every aspect of Christmas, from the plum pudding to the ornaments to hang on the tree, to gifts to make for all the family. For some projects you'll need to be handy with a needle; others just need scissors, glue, and a little patience. Many projects are suitable for children to try. Little ones will love decorating cookies or helping to make gingerbread men, while older children may like to make their own wrapping paper or Christmas cards.*

If you're planning an informal party, you'll find recipes for delicious drinks and traditional mince pies. For a more formal dinner, try your hand at creating a special centerpiece and some stunning table linens. To decorate the house itself there are ingenious ideas for displaying seasonal evergreens, plus swags and wreaths made from more durable materials that you'll be able to bring out year after year.

We're not suggesting that you attempt to do it all, there are bound to be elements that you'd rather buy than make, but even in the busiest lifestyle, it's possible to find a few moments to stitch some simple lavender sachets or to spice up a bottle of olive oil with chilies or rosemary. Give free rein to your creativity, and have a merry Christmas.

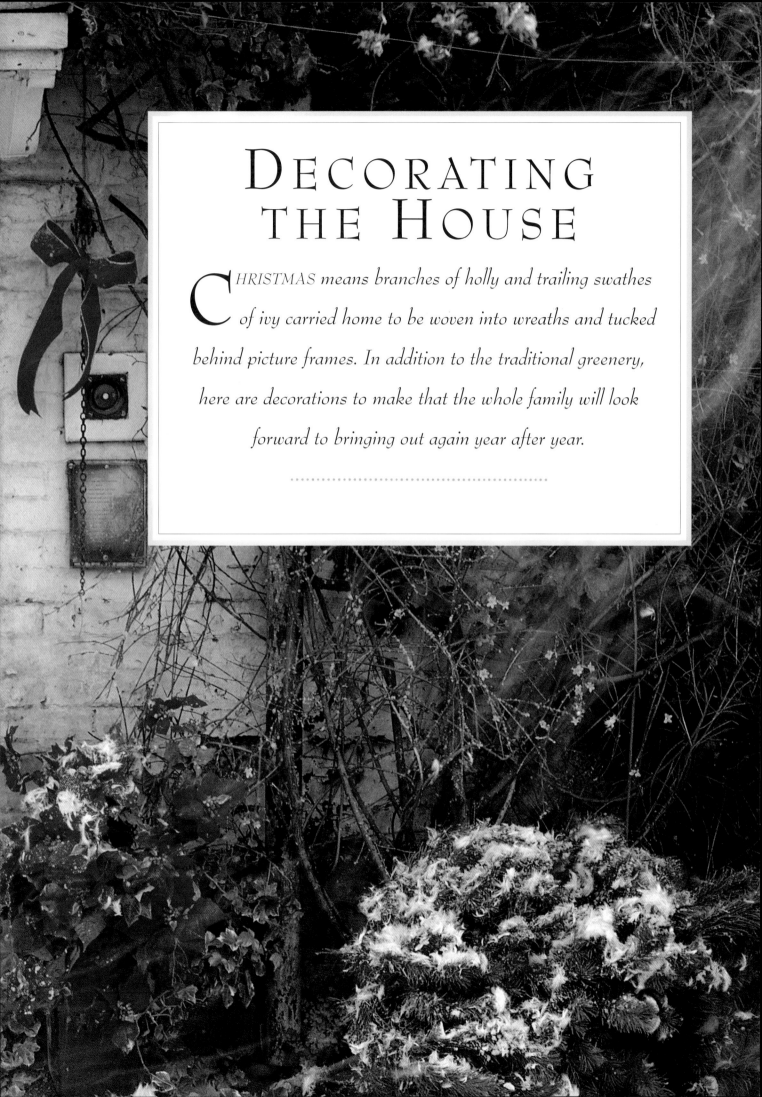

DECORATING THE HOUSE

C HRISTMAS *means branches of holly and trailing swathes of ivy carried home to be woven into wreaths and tucked behind picture frames. In addition to the traditional greenery, here are decorations to make that the whole family will look forward to bringing out again year after year.*

CHRISTMAS WREATH

A TRADITIONAL Christmas wreath for the front door will welcome visitors to your home throughout the season. The traditional evergreens – holly and ivy – are entwined with pine cones and highlighted with clusters of gold bells in this simple yet professional-looking design. The wreath base is bought ready made from a florist's shop. Wire in the foliage, following the step-by-step guide. Artificial berries are a good way of adding extra color and contrast, and are hard to tell from the real thing – ideal if your holly is less than well endowed.

MATERIALS

20 in. (50 cm) diameter wreath base
Medium-gauge florist's wire
12 bunches of ivy
6 bunches of variegated holly
6 sprigs of small artificial berries
4 bunches of mistletoe
9 pine cones, lightly sprayed white
3-5 sprigs of dark green holly; 3-5 sprigs of artificial berries
30 in. (75 cm) length of gold ribbon, ½ in. (12 mm) wide
9 small gold bells

Left: Gold bows and glossy evergreens are perfect partners in this Christmas wreath. Don't forget the essential sprigs of mistletoe.

1 Take 4-5 sprigs of ivy and wire together with medium-gauge florist's wire, leaving enough wire to fasten the ivy to the wreath. Make 12 bunches.

2 Fasten the ivy bunches to the wreath by twisting the wire around the twigs in the base. All the bunches should face the same way.

3 Continue until the base is completely covered with ivy, overlapping the bunches to hide the wires and to avoid leaving large gaps.

4 Make up 6 bunches using sprigs of variegated holly 6 in. (15 cm) in length and artificial berries and wire them to the base, spacing them evenly.

5 Make up 4 bunches of mistletoe by wiring together 5-6 sprigs 9 in. (22.5cm) in length, then wire them to the base, spacing them evenly.

6 Wrap medium-gauge florist's wire around the base of each pine cone and twist to secure. Make 3 clusters of 3 cones each and wire them to the wreath.

8 Attach these holly and berry bunches to the wreath wherever a splash of extra color is needed. Wire them in carefully as the wreath is getting quite awkward to handle now.

7 Take a 5 in. (12.5 cm) sprig of dark green holly and a sprig of large artificial berries and wire together. Make between 3 and 5 bunches.

9 Cut the gold ribbon into three equal lengths and trim the ends to stop them fraying. Thread 3 bells onto each piece and tie in a neat bow.

10 Push medium-gauge florist's wire through the loops of the bells and twist to secure. Attach the bell clusters to the wreath, spacing them out evenly.

ADVENT CALENDAR

A STORE-BOUGHT *cork bulletin board is the starting point for this colorful and charming children's advent calendar. As each day begins, a felt "door" is taken away from the Christmas tree to reveal the image below. Map pins have been used to secure the doors, and as each one is "opened" it can be shifted and used to decorate the space around the tree. Using pins also makes it easy to reuse the calendar, and attaching the images with double-sided tape means that they can be changed every year.*

MATERIALS

Framed cork bulletin board, about 12 x 17 in. (30 x 43 cm)
Gold paint
Paint brush
Scissors
Stiff paper; Double-sided tape
Red tissue paper
Felt in two shades of green, and red and yellow
Glitter pens; Clear glue
Red embroidery floss and needle
Red and gold glitter pens
Small, images from old magazines, postcards, stamps, etc.
Map pins

Right: A fun and imaginative advent calendar will make sure that the days leading up to Christmas are extra-special for children.

1 Paint the frame of the bulletin board in gold, without worrying too much if you splash paint onto the cork. Leave the frame to dry and cut a piece of stiff paper that will fit snugly inside the frame.

2 Lay the stiff paper on a sheet of red tissue. Fold the surplus over to the back, then slot the covered paper into the frame of the bulletin board.

3 Use the template on page 145 to cut out the segments of the Christmas tree in two shades of green felt. Arrange them so that they overlap, and glue the overlapping sections together neatly.

4 When the glue is completely dry, make a decorative border for the tree by slip-stitching around the edge in red embroidery thread.

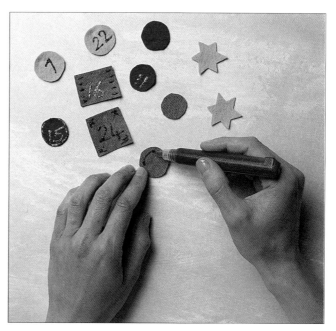

5 Cut 24 very simple shapes from colored felt to form the advent calendars "doors" – squares and circles are easiest, but you could also try cutting stars.

6 Embellish the felt "doors" with glitter pens and number each one. Allow them to dry before matching them to the cut-out images (see next step).

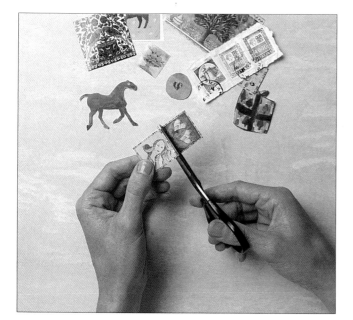

7 Cut out 24 appealing images from old magazines, cards, wrapping paper, even postage stamps. Remember to match shapes and sizes to the felt doors you have already cut.

8 Use double-sided tape to attach the images and pin the covers on top, spacing them randomly on the tree. Decorate the calendar further using any leftover scraps of felt.

FIREPLACE GARLAND

THIS ATTRACTIVE garland is made almost entirely from dried and artificial leaves and flowers, so it will hold its shape and color for weeks. Dried grapevine, readily available from florist's shops, forms the base, and the method described makes a garland around nine feet (three meters) long; measure your fireplace before you buy the vine and adjust the length accordingly. Artificial white roses and hellebores were used to contrast with the poinsettias and red leaves. There is no need to copy this combination slavishly, you can substitute any light-colored flowers of a similar size. Once you have hung the garland above the fireplace, make any last-minute adjustments to cover gaps or awkwardly placed pieces.

MATERIALS

9 foot (3 meter) length of dried grape vine
A glue gun; Medium-gauge florist's wire
Wired gold ribbon, 2¼ in. (6 cm) wide
Artificial flowers: 9 poinsettias, 12 white hellebores,
4 white roses
10-15 sprigs of red and green artificial leaves
14-16 dried hydrangeas
8 larch or other large cones, sprayed gold
8 yellow and 2 brown paper roses
1 bunch of Chinese lanterns; 6 sprigs of artificial red berries
4 bunches mistletoe; 6 bunches variegated ivy

1 Wet the dried vine and stretch to the required shape on a piece of board, securing with a nail in each corner. Leave for a day or two.

2 Push 14 in. (35 cm) of florist's wire through one top corner, bend it and twist the ends to form a loop. Repeat at the other corner.

3 Tie 36 in. (90 cm) of wired gold ribbon around one top corner of the garland, without covering or obstructing the wire loop.

4 Tie the ribbon into a neat bow. Repeat the process using the remaining length of ribbon for the opposite corner of the garland.

5 Use a glue gun to fix a large poinsettia in the middle of the top of the garland. Press it lightly with your fingertips until secure.

6 Place a small poinsettia head on either side of the large one and glue them into position in exactly the same way.

7 Glue a large poinsettia head under each corner bow and smaller heads halfway down and at the bottom of each side of the garland.

8 Place a white hellebore flower on either side of the large poinsettia head at the top of the garland and glue in position.

9 Continue building up the central motif by placing a white rose under each white hellebore and gluing them into position.

10 Then, on each side, glue a white hellebore and a white rose on either side of the corner poinsettia and a white hellebore under the middle poinsettia.

11 On each side of the top of the garland, glue a white hellebore halfway between the central motif and the corner.

12 Glue sprigs of artificial red leaves between the central motif and each corner, working the leaves in among the twiggy vine stems for a natural effect.

13 Glue 2 dried hydrangea heads above the central motif. Choose heads that still retain a strong hint of color for the best results.

14 Glue the rest of the hydrangea heads around the garland, distributing them evenly but without trying to arrange them too consciously symmetrically.

15 Glue 1 cone on either side of the central motif and 3 down each side of the garland. As the cones are heavy, glue both stalks and cones.

16 Glue a yellow rose on either side of the central motif. Glue 2 yellow roses and 1 brown rose halfway down each side, and a single yellow rose at the bottom.

18 Insert a few artificial green leaves for contrast. Then take 4 bunches of berried mistletoe and glue in a fan shape under the central motif.

17 Glue 4 to 5 small sprigs of Chinese lanterns to each side, spacing them fairly evenly. Add sprigs of artificial berries wherever you think extra color is needed.

19 Finally, take 6 small bunches of variegated ivy. Glue 1 bunch on either side of the mistletoe, 1 in each corner, and 1 halfway down each side.

ORANGE POMANDERS

P OMANDERS *have been popular for hundreds of years. The simplest sort, studded with cloves, were carried as far back as the sixteenth century, when it was hoped they would ward off illness. These decorative variations on the classic pomander use the traditional cloves to form patterns of spirals, diamonds and stars. For best results, start making your pomanders several weeks before Christmas to give them time to dry out a little.*

MATERIALS

*Small, thin-skinned oranges
(blood oranges are ideal)
Cloves
Sharp kitchen knife*

1 Push lines of cloves into an orange to divide it into eight segments and make long slits in the orange between the lines of cloves. Or use the cloves to create simple swirls and star patterns.

2 To dry the pomanders, put them in a cool oven and leave the door open.

LINOCUT POMANDERS

*C*UTTING INTO *the white pith of oranges and other citrus fruit to create a contrasting pattern is a simple yet satisfying way of decorating them. You don't need to dry these pomanders in an oven; they will dry out naturally as they sit on display to become permanent decorations. An artist's linocutting or wood carving tools make easy work of cutting the pattern – just remember to point the blade of the tool away from you at all times.*

MATERIALS

Fresh oranges with firm skins
Black felt pen
Artist's linocutting or wood
carving tools

1 Use the black felt pen to draw a pattern onto an orange. Start off with an easy design to begin with, until you become more adept.

2 Cut out the pattern with the lino tool, following the lines exactly, so that you don't leave any ink on the orange's skin.

IVY STREAMERS

THESE IVY-AND-RIBBON streamers are a novel solution to the perennial problem of how to display vast numbers of Christmas cards each year. The idea is easily adapted for other features in a room or hallway, too. Instead of framing the doorway, you could use the materials to make a decorative swag for a mantel or banister. If you pin the cards carefully to the streamers, you may even find that you can reuse the veiling and the chiffon ribbon over and over again.

MATERIALS

Long strands of ivy
Reel wire
Two 12 in. (30 cm) sprigs of variegated holly with berries
6 dried pomegranate shells, sprayed gold
Medium-gauge florist's wire
Two 32 in. (80 cm) lengths of wired blue-green chiffon ribbon, 1½ in. (4 cm) wide
Two 18 in. (45 cm) lengths of wired red ribbon, 2½ in. (6 cm) wide
Two pieces of veiling or white net, 4 in. (10 cm) wide, approximately the same length as the height of the door
Two pieces of wired blue-green chiffon ribbon, 1½ in. (4 cm) wide, approximately the same length as the height of the door

Left: Decorate a doorway with Christmas cards pinned to gauzy twists of net and ribbon, set against seasonal streamers of ivy.

1 Drape ivy around the door, securing at the top and corners by gently tapping tacks into the door frame. Wire in extra ivy using reel wire.

2 Continue until you have covered the entire length of the door. Gently tweak the leaves so that as many as possible face forward.

3 Lay 2 sprigs of variegated holly together, cut ends overlapping. Wire them together and then wire them to the center of the ivy above the door.

4 Make a small hole in the side of each dried pomegranate. Push through a length of florist's wire and bend one end back flat against the fruit.

5 Hold 3 wired pomegranates together firmly, then twist a length of florist's wire around the stems and between each fruit to make a secure bunch. Repeat.

6 Take a 32 in. (80 cm) length of wired blue-green ribbon and twist it around the pomegranates. Tie in a four-looped bow (instructions on page 140). Repeat this step.

7 Take an 18 in. (45 cm) length of wired red ribbon and tie in a two-looped bow (instructions on page 140). Attach behind the pomegranate bunch. Repeat this step.

8 Take one length of veiling and one of blue-green ribbon, tie them together and hang down one side of the door. Repeat for the other side.

9 Loosely twist the lengths of veiling and ribbon over each other and knot at the base. Fix a pomegranate bunch to each corner of the door frame.

10 Using dress-making pins, pin Christmas cards down the length of the ribbon twists. If you have very young children, glue the cards in place.

PAPERCUT GARLANDS

G*ARLANDS CUT from paper are a popular method of decoration in Poland and Switzerland. Try the pattern below, then experiment with your own designs for Christmas.*

MATERIALS

White paper, 7 x 28½ in. (18 x 72 cm)
Tracing paper; Card
Scissors; Pencil
Cutting mat
Craft knife
Clear glue
Selection of sequins

Opposite: Figures and animals lend their shapes well to the time-honored art of cutting decorative garlands from paper.

1 Fold the paper concertina-style, to produce 9 sections, each 3½ in. (9 cm) wide. Trace the template on page 149 onto a piece of card and draw around the tree onto the folded paper.

2 Place the paper on the cutting mat and cut away the excess paper. Don't cut around the three lowest branches and the base as these points hold the garland together.

3 Unfold the garland and decorate the trees with silver sequins. Put dabs of glue onto the tree to hold each sequin in place.

ROSE WREATH

THIS UNUSUAL *heart-shaped wreath is lightly scented with the warm, subtle fragrance of rose oil. Made entirely from artificial leaves and flowers, it will last for years and become a treasured favorite. Imitation ivy has the advantage of being easy to bend and twist and, of course, it won't dry out and die. The wreath will make an elegant addition to any internal door; don't be tempted to try to hang it outside, though, as it is far too delicate to withstand the elements.*

MATERIALS

48 in. (120 cm) fencing wire
Cotton thread; Gutta-percha
Length of artificial ivy at least 48 in. (120 cm) long
Length of artificial pine cones at least 48 in. (120 cm) long
3 sprigs artificial berries; 3 artificial roses
Rose oil; Medium-gauge florist's wire
Artificial bird, sprayed gold
2 yds. (2 m) wired pink chiffon ribbon, 1½ in. (4 cm) wide

1 Draw a large heart to use as a template, then bend the fencing wire in the middle to form the point at the base of the heart.

Opposite: Artificial roses can look very realistic. Small rosebuds are ideal for this wreath – heavier flowers would unbalance the overall effect.

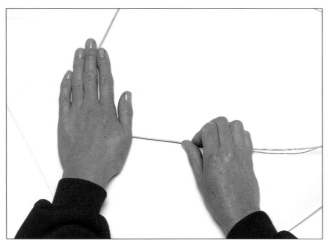

2 Following your template, gradually bend the wire into the heart shape, working your way around from the bottom to the top of the heart.

3 Overlap the wires at the top of the heart and bind them firmly together with cotton thread, knotting the ends firmly before cutting them off.

4 Wrap gutta-percha around the heart-shaped frame, making sure you cover the wire completely. Gutta-percha is self adhesive so no glue is needed.

5 Next wind the artificial ivy around the frame. Adjust the leaves as you work so that they fan out and hide the gutta-percha as far as possible.

6 Wind the length of artificial pine cones around the frame. (Or wire 6 individual pairs of gold-sprayed cones to the wreath instead.)

7 Space the berry sprigs evenly around the wreath and attach them by twisting their stems. Hide the ends of the stems under the ivy leaves.

8 Using a dropper or a very fine paint brush, coat the inner petals of each artificial rose with rose oil.

9 Space the roses evenly around the wreath, roughly halfway between the sprigs of berries, and attach them by twisting their stems around the frame.

10 Use florists's wire to attach the bird to the top of the wreath, binding it firmly in place. Cover the wire with a piece of gutta-percha.

11 Loop the ribbon around the top of the wreath, making sure it is properly centered. Knot the ends just above the frame, behind the bird.

12 To make a loop for hanging the wreath, tie another knot 9 in. (23 cm) from the first one. Then tie the two loose ends of the ribbon in a bow.

13 Tie the two loose ends of the bow into another bow that lies diagonally across the first one. Trim the ends of the ribbon to neaten.

DECORATING
THE TREE

C HILDREN LOVE *helping to decorate the Christmas tree. The box of decorations brought down from the attic always seems to hold a few extra surprises. Here are some additions to the familiar baubles and lights: most will last a lifetime, others will doubtless disappear during the twelve days of Christmas.*

LEAFY ALUMINUM GARLAND

*S*PARKLING *oak leaves make a festive garland for the distinctive needles of a blue spruce Christmas tree. The leaves are cut from aluminum, the easiest to use of all metal foils.*

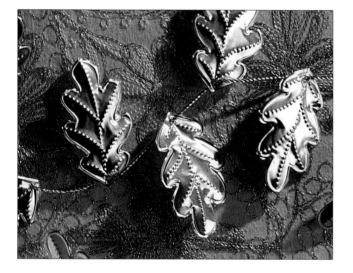

MATERIALS

Tracing paper
Roll of aluminum foil, 6½ in. (16.5 cm) wide
Wad of folded tissue paper
Empty ballpoint pen (i.e., with no ink left)
Dressmaker's tracing wheel; Small, pointed scissors
Awl; 2¼ yd. (2 m) silver cord

Opposite: Shimmering white lights are reflected in the shiny metal surface of the aluminum leaves and a scattering of silver baubles.

1 Using tracing paper, copy the template on page 149. Place the aluminum foil on the tissue paper to protect your work surface and draw 20 leaves with the ballpoint pen.

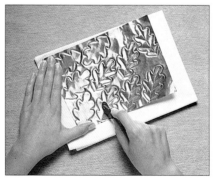

2 Make the pattern of the leaf veins with the dressmaker's wheel. Cut out each leaf about ⅛ in. (2 mm) beyond its outline.

3 Use the awl to make a hole in each leaf for the cord. Make the garland as long as you like, adding one leaf every 4 in. (10 cm).

TREE ANGEL

N*O SELF-RESPECTING Christmas tree would be complete without an angel on the topmost branch. Conveniently, this angel is made mostly from felt, which can be glued, rather than sewn, if you prefer. The skirt is hollow so that she can sit easily on the tree, and can be decorated with beads or tinsel. Clasped in her hands is a felt heart, a suitable Christmas symbol, and the wings are edged in blanket stitch for a homespun touch.*

MATERIALS

Tracing paper
Pencil
Scissors
White, pink, and yellow or orange felt
Small piece of calico or unbleached cotton fabric
Gold thread
Needle
Wadding
Sewing machine
Fabric glue
Thick, blonde-colored embroidery floss
Colored pencils
Gold bugle beads

Opposite: A harmonious trio of angels for the Christmas tree, easily made from felt or scraps of cloth.

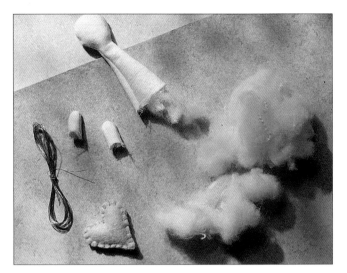

1 Copy the templates, opposite, for the angel's gown, heart, wings, head, and hands. Use them to cut out 2 gowns from white felt, 2 hearts from pink felt, and 2 pairs of wings from orange or yellow felt. Cut the head and neck twice from calico and cut out 4 hands from calico. Take the 2 wing pieces and sew them together, using gold thread and a blanket stitch. Add extra random stitches to the wings for decoration.

2 Take the 2 hearts and stitch them together, again using gold thread and a blanket stitch. Leave a small opening, and stuff the heart with wadding. Pack it in tightly, then close the opening with a blanket stitch. Pin the head and neck pieces together with right sides facing. Machine stitch around the edge, leaving an opening at the bottom. Turn the head right side out and stuff with wadding. Stitch the opening closed. Make the hands in a similar way.

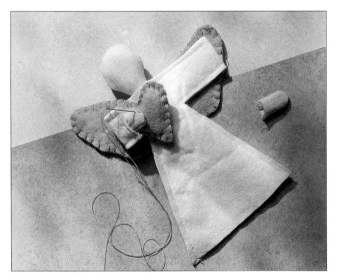

3 To make the gown, place the 2 pieces of felt together and machine stitch along the sides and sleeves, leaving gaps for the neck and hands. Sew the neck of the angel's head into the gown, catching it in with tiny, almost invisible, stitches. Sew the hands into the sleeve holes, then sew the heart to the hands. Stitch the wings to the back of the gown.

4 Spread glue on top of the head and add rows of thick embroidery floss to make the hair. Draw in the mouth, eyes and cheeks with colored pencils. Trim the felt gown by sewing on a scattering of gold bugle beads or adding a border of festive gold tinsel.

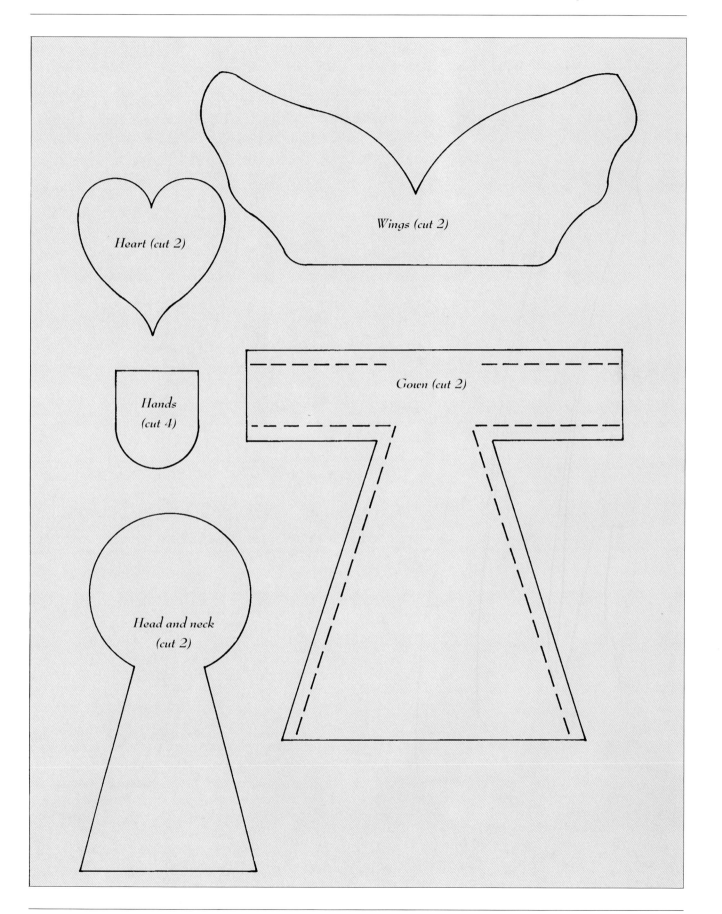

Heart (cut 2)

Wings (cut 2)

Hands
(cut 4)

Gown (cut 2)

Head and neck
(cut 2)

TREE STOCKINGS

F ELT IS THE *ideal fabric for making these tree stockings – no need to worry about hems or fraying. Fill them with small toys for children, or foil-wrapped chocolates for adults, before you hang them on the tree.*

Left: Gold-spotted felt is so pretty in its own right that additional decoration was kept to a minimum on this miniature tree stocking.

1 Trace the template on page 144 and cut out 2 stocking pieces in red felt. Stitch together, leaving the top open. Tie off any loose threads.

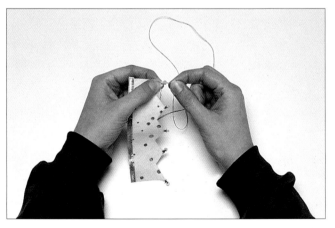

2 Cut one cuff from white felt, fold in four, and cut a "V" into the bottom edge. Open out and stitch gold ribbon along the top.

3 Stitch a pearl bead to each point, then sew cuff to the top of the stocking, aligning the open ends with the back seam.

4 Fold the ribbon in half and stitch it to the top back seam to form a loop. Tie the loose ends in a bow.

MINI WREATH

T*HIS MINIATURE wreath is made from artificial leaves and berries, and dried flowers; wrap it in tissue and store it carefully and you will be able to use it year after year.*

MATERIALS

18 in. (45 cm) length of red ribbon, ¼ in. (6 mm) wide
4 in. (10 cm) wreath base, available from florist's shops
All-purpose glue
3 small red ribbon bows
4 small bunches of artificial berries
Artificial green leaves
Small dried flowers, such as individual hydrangea flowers, sprayed silver and gold

Left: Add extra color to your miniature wreath by gluing on some ribbon curls (instructions on page 141).

1 Make a loop at one end of the ribbon and secure with a single stitch. Wind ribbon around the wreath base and glue in place. Glue on the 3 ribbon bows.

2 Position the bunches of artificial berries and green leaves at equal distances around the wreath base and then glue them in place.

3 Make sure that the wreath base is completely covered by gluing on dried hydrangea flowers sprayed gold and silver wherever there is a gap.

CHRISTMAS COOKIES

*C*HILDREN WILL *enjoy decorating these stars and snowmen.*
Eat them within a week of making, if they last that long!

For the cookies:
⅛ cup butter
3 tablespoons superfine sugar
2 tablespoons cornstarch
⅝ cup plain flour

Preheat the oven to 300°F. Cream together the butter and half the sugar in a mixing bowl until light and fluffy. Fold in the cornstarch, and then the remaining sugar.

Press the mixture into a 7 x 10 in. (17.5 x 25 cm) baking pan. Cover with parchment paper and a layer of dried beans and bake blind for around 30 minutes. When cool enough to handle, cut into shapes and place on a rack. Decorate the cookies before they get cold.

For the glaze icing:
1 cup confectioner's sugar
6 tablespoons warm water

To decorate the star cookies:
Chocolate chips; Silver balls
To decorate the snowmen:
Silver balls; Angelica; Chocolate chips
Flaked coconut; Marzipan
Red and green food coloring

You will also need:
8 in. (20 cm) lengths of ribbon, ¼ in. (6 mm) wide
Drinking straws

1 Cut up the drinking straws and push a short length into the top of each cookie to make a hole for the ribbon. Leave the straw in place.

2 Put a small amount of glaze on each cookie. Working quickly before the cookies cool, spread the icing evenly over the top and sides using a knife.

3 Add chocolate chips and silver balls before the icing sets. Leave to cool. To allow the icing to harden, store cookies in an airtight tin for a couple of days.

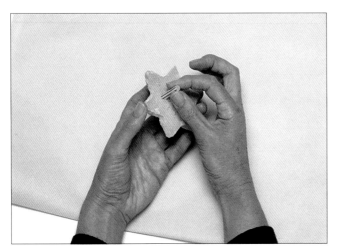

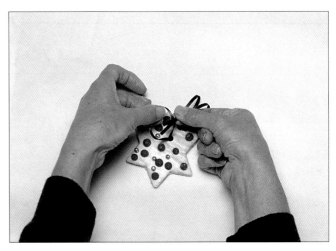

4 To remove the drinking straws, push them from the front of the cookie through to the back. Pulling them out from the front risks cracking the icing.

5 Fold a piece of ribbon in half and push it through the hole in the cookie from back to front. Thread the cut ends through the loop and pull up tight.

6 Tie the cut ends into a loop to hang the cookie. Trim any excess ribbon on the diagonal to neaten.

SNOWMEN

1 Cut out the snowmen and insert drinking straws (see page 47). Ice the cookies and add the decorations. Sprinkle with dessicated coconut.

2 Tint a small piece of marzipan with red food coloring and blend until the color is evenly mixed. Colour another piece green.

3 Roll out the green marzipan and cut out a scarf measuring ½ x 6 in. (1.5 x 15 cm). Cut tiny strips of red marzipan and lay them on it diagonally, pressing in position.

4 Turn the scarf over and trim off the ends of red marzipan. Remove the drinking straws from the cookies (see page 47).

5 Drape the scarf around the snowman's neck, crossing the ends at the front. Press the marzipan scarf to hold it in place. Tie a ribbon loop through the hole left by the straw.

DOUGH
ORNAMENTS

S ALT DOUGH *is ideal for making decorations. All the*

ingredients and utensils that you will need are already in your

kitchen, and the dough can be mixed and ready to use in minutes.

······································

<table>
<tr><th colspan="1">MATERIALS</th></tr>
</table>

2 ½ cups plain flour, 1 ¼ cups salt, and 1 cup water for the dough
2 flat-sided baking trays
Selection of cookie cutters
Sharp vegetable knife
Garlic press; Pastry brush; Rolling pin; Cocktail stick
Poster paints; Gold felt-tip pen
Matte varnish

Mix the flour and salt together thoroughly. Add half the water and mix until smooth. Then add the rest of the water, a little at a time, until all the ingredients bind to a dough. Roll out on a floured work surface to ¼ in. (6 mm) thick and cut out shapes.

Wipe the baking tray with a damp cloth and transfer the shapes, arranging them so that they don't touch. Add the decorative details and use a cocktail stick to make a hole for a loop to hang them.

Bake the decorations in the oven at 250°F for 24 hours. When they are completely dry they will easily lift off the baking tray. Leave them to cool in the oven overnight if possible, to avoid cracking. If children are helping to make the ornaments, be sure they know that you can't eat salt dough!

Turn the page for more tips and ideas on decorating your tree ornaments.

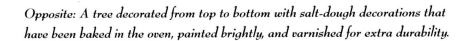

Opposite: A tree decorated from top to bottom with salt-dough decorations that have been baked in the oven, painted brightly, and varnished for extra durability.

Use leftover scraps of dough to decorate the basic shapes, attaching the decorations before baking.

Improve upon the basic cookie-cutter shapes by adding detailed seasonal decorations.

A snowman is made from two balls of dough. Elongate one for the body and fix together with a drop of water. Use two strips of dough joined on either side of the neck for a scarf.

String, raffia, or ribbon make ideal loops to hang the decorations. Use a generous length to make them easy to hang.

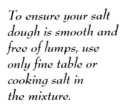

All the modeling tools you need can be found in the kitchen. Sculpt decorations with knives, scissors, even cocktail sticks.

Children's thick tempera paints are perfectly suited to decorating salt doughs – watercolors are too pale.

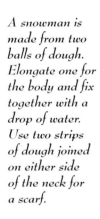

Finishing decorations with two coats of matte varnish prevents moisture from penetrating and spoiling them.

To ensure your salt dough is smooth and free of lumps, use only fine table or cooking salt in the mixture.

This jolly Santa Claus features pom-poms made from small balls of dough attached with water.

Children will enjoy making their own decorations. The dough is cheap to make, so don't worry about mistakes.

Pressing dough through a garlic press is an easy way to create hair. Cut off the resulting strands with a sharp knife.

Basic colors work best. Paint the decorations in bold reds, blues, yellows, and greens, with a touch of black and white.

Dusting the cookie cutter with flour prevents the shape from distorting when the cutter is pressed into the dough.

Working with the dough can dry out your skin because of the salt content, so you might want to wear rubber gloves.

This angel's head is made from a flattened ball, while knife cuts were used to create the folds in the gown.

Remember, baking is the most important part of creating your dough decorations — never attempt to rush things.

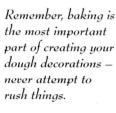

To store decorations, wrap them in tissue paper and keep in a warm place so that they don't get damp.

SCENTED SACHETS

THESE TINY *sachets are decorated with cross-stitch motifs. Fill them with dried lavender or make your own citrus-scented potpourri by mixing together the ingredients listed and leaving them in a cool, dark place for a few weeks to mature.*

MATERIALS

10 count Aida fabric	*For the citrus potpourri:*
Embroidery thread; Needle; Scissors	*1 pint (500 ml) mixed scented leaves such as thyme,*
Muslin; Dried lavender; Beads	*rosemary, marjoram, scented geranium, or lemon balm*
12 in. (30 cm) length of ribbon, ¼ in. (5 mm) wide	*1 oz. (25 g) orris root powder; 1 oz. (25 g) dried lavender*
14 in. (35 cm) length of ribbon, ¼ in. (5 mm) wide	*Small pieces of orange, lemon or grapefruit peel*
7 in. (17.5 cm) length of ribbon, ¼ in. (5 mm) wide	*4-6 drops lemon oil*

Opposite: The ribbon trimmings and hanging loops echo the colors of the cross-stitch embroidery in these pretty scented sachets.

1 Cross stitch a motif from pages 56-57 on a 2½ in. (6 cm) square of 10-count Aida fabric and add some beads. Overcast to prevent fraying.

2 Turn over the raw edges and press with your fingertips to flatten them. Machine stitch in place and tie off loose threads.

3 Cut a 3 x 6 in. (7.5 x 15 cm) piece of muslin and fold it in half to form a square. Stitch along three sides and turn inside out.

6 Machine stitch a ribbon border around the sachet, leaving a small loop in each corner. Stitch a decorative bead into each corner.

7 Fold in half the long length of ribbon for the loop. Stitch to the sachet. Place the shorter length diagonally across it and stitch in place.

4 Trim the open end to neaten, then sew the muslin to the back of the cross-stitched motif, leaving the open end of the sachet unstitched.

5 Fold under the raw edge of the muslin. Fill the sachet with dried lavender or potpourri and tack down the open edge.

8 Tie the short length of ribbon in a bow. Tie the loose ends of the loop in a second bow so that it lies diagonally across it.

DRIED APPLE SPRAYS

MOST OF THE *ingredients in these dried apple sprays can be found around the home and garden. Quick and easy to produce, they make an effective and natural-looking tree or package decoration.*

> ### MATERIALS
>
> *2 dried apple slices (see page 142); 3 artificial berries with stems*
> *3-4 sprigs of small evergreen leaves, 5 in. (12.5 cm) long,*
> *sprayed gold; Thin gold ribbon or twine, 4 in. (10 cm) long*
> *All-purpose clear glue*
> *2 small gold ribbon curls (see page 141)*
> *20 in. (50 cm) length of wired blue-green chiffon ribbon*
> *Florist's wire*

1 Thread a 6 in. (15 cm) length of florist's wire through the needle holes in the apple slices, leaving an equal amount of wire on each side. Twist the wires together.

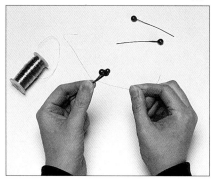

2 Take three artificial berries and wrap wire around their stems to wire them into a bunch. Leave about 3 in. (7.5 cm) of wire protruding.

3 Place the berries on top of the apple slices, holding the berry stems and apple wires in one hand. Wrap wire around the berry stems and apple wires to bind them together.

4 Place the leaf sprigs behind the apples and berries. Hold a gold twine loop behind the leaves. Use the wire from the berries to bind everything together.

5 Place two tiny dabs of glue on the front of the spray and press on the ribbon curls. Leave to dry.

6 Tie a wired blue-green chiffon ribbon bow around the top of the spray, taking care to hide the stalks and wire. Trim the ribbon ends on the diagonal to neaten.

DECORATING THE TABLE

THE COMBINATION of fine food and a magnificently decorated table help to make Christmas dinner truly memorable. In this chapter you'll find instructions for a traditional holly and ivy centerpiece to form the focal point of the table, plus ideas for linen, place settings, and tabletop trees.

CITRUS CHRISTMAS TREE

I F YOU DON'T *have space for a traditional Christmas tree or can't face sweeping up dropped pine needles every day, then this little tabletop tree is a colorful alternative. All the miniature fruit and leaves are artificial so there's no mess to clean up: it also means you can use the tree again and again. Artificial fruit and leaves are readily available in department stores and garden centers; here they are supplemented by curls of dried citrus peel (see page 142) that give the tree a fresh natural scent.*

MATERIALS

6 in. (15 cm) diameter terra-cotta pot, sprayed gold
Florist's clay
1 dry oasis cone, 12 in. (30 cm) high and 4 in. (10 cm) in diameter at base
Scalpel
4-5 birch twigs, about 6-8 in. (15-20 cm) in length
1 block of dry oasis
Lichen moss
25-30 artificial poinsettia leaves, lightly sprayed with a little gold paint

Glue gun
All-purpose glue
A selection of artificial miniature fruit and berries such as peaches, plums, apples, red berries, rose hips
Medium-gauge florist's wire
Curls of dried citrus peel (see page 142)
Gold ribbon curls (see page 141)
Gold star, 3 in. (7.5 cm) high
30 in. (75 cm) length of wired gold chiffon ribbon, 3 in. (7.5 cm) wide

Opposite: An opulently decorated tree composed of fruits and leaves, that will sit attractively on a table or windowsill at Christmas.

1 Take a small block of florist's clay and knead it in your hands until it is soft and pliable enough to be molded into the shape of the flower pot.

2 Press the clay into the pot. It should come at least one third of the way up to make a firm foundation. The clay will set hard within a couple of days.

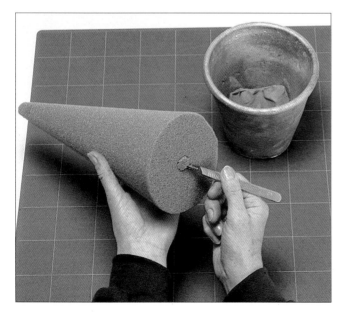

3 Using a scalpel, cut a small hole about 1½ in. (4 cm) deep in the base of the oasis cone to take the birch twigs that will form the tree's trunk.

4 Push the thickest birch twig into the oasis. Make sure that the cone is firmly wedged onto the twig and the birch twig is in the center of the cone.

5 Push thinner twigs into the oasis cone around the main twig to create a really sturdy trunk. Wedge the trunk firmly into the florist's clay at the bottom of the pot.

6 Cut small pieces from an oasis block and use them to fill in around the trunk, pushing them firmly down into the pot. Keep the trunk and cone vertical as you work.

7 Spread some lichen moss around the base of the trunk to disguise the oasis and give the impression of a real pot of soil. Now you are ready to decorate the cone.

8 Starting from the bottom of the oasis cone and gradually working upwards use the glue gun to attach the artificial poinsettia leaves, overlapping the leaves slightly as you add them.

9 Continue until you have completely covered the oasis cone with poinsettia leaves, but don't pack them too tightly together or you may find it difficult to add the fruit at the next stage.

10 Start adding the plums, spacing them randomly around the tree and using a glue gun to fix them in place. Position heavier fruit at the base to prevent the tree from looking top heavy.

11 To attach bunches of peaches, bend a short length of medium-gauge florist's wire in half to form a pin and push it over the stem of the fruit and into the oasis cone.

12 Attach clusters of apples randomly around the tree. Stand back from your work every now and then to check that you are keeping the tree's conical shape as you add more and more fruit.

13 Insert red berries and sprigs of rose hips evenly over the tree. Don't overdo the berries and hips: red is a dominant color that could overwhelm the tree if you are heavy-handed.

14 Check that the tree is still vertical and not leaning to one side. Then add the citrus peel and gold ribbon curls, allowing the ribbon to drop naturally around the fruit and foliage.

15 Take the gold star and glue it securely to the top of the tree, aligning one point of the star with the very tip of the tree so that it points upward.

16 Put a dab of glue on the back of the pot and attach the gold ribbon just under the rim, tying it in a neat two-looped bow (see page 140).

FAN-SHAPED TREE

HERE IS *another idea for an alternative Christmas tree, this time inspired it is by sophisticated but essentially simple Japanese flower arrangements. The materials can all be gathered from the garden and are largely used in a natural state, apart from the merest hint of gold and silver paint used to enhance some of the money plant and birch twigs. The natural rustic feel is reinforced by using coarse burlap to cover the flowerpot base. The color scheme is limited, allowing the vibrant orange Chinese lanterns to catch the eye.*

....

MATERIALS

4 in. (10 cm) diameter terra-cotta pot
Florist's clay
14 x 14 in. (35 x 35 cm) piece of burlap
Glue gun
All-purpose glue
1 bunch of natural birch twigs
1 bunch of birch twigs, sprayed silvery-white
1 bunch of Chinese lanterns
1 bunch of natural money plant
1 bunch of money plant, sprayed gold
18 in. (45 cm) length of green paper ribbon

Opposite: Bring a corner of the room to life with a bold, fan-shaped arrangement of money plant, Chinese lanterns and birch twigs.

1 Put the florist's clay in the bottom of the pot and press down firmly. Unlike oasis, florist's clay does not crumble and will set hard in a couple of days.

2 Round off the burlap square by cutting away the corners. Place the pot in the middle and, using a glue gun, dab glue around the inside top edge of the pot.

3 Fold the burlap up over the rim of the pot, gathering it evenly as you go, and pressing it firmly against the patches of glue until it is firmly stuck.

4 Position one natural birch twig in the middle of the pot, pressing it down into the clay. Place four or five more birch twigs loosely around it, to establish the basic fan shape.

5 Insert 8-10 silvery-white birch twigs between the natural twigs. Try to distribute them evenly so that the arrangement looks balanced. The twigs should be roughly the same length.

6 Insert 3-4 sprigs of Chinese lanterns at the front of the arrangement. Don't be tempted to add too many: the color is very strong and the arrangement could easily look garish.

7 Insert 3-4 stems of natural money plant, distributing them evenly throughout the arrangement. The use of these semitransparent papery seed pods forms an effective contrast to the hard lines of the birch twigs.

8 Insert 6-8 stems of gold money plant, again distributing them evenly throughout the arrangement. Adding a hint of gold subtly reinforces the warm hues of the Chinese lanterns without overpowering them.

9 Trim the twigs and stems if necessary, to stop the arrangement looking too untidy. If you spot any obvious gaps, fill them with leftover sprigs of any materials that remain.

10 To finish the fan-shaped tree, tie a length of rough-textured green paper ribbon around the center of the pot. Fasten it with a double knot and tweak the ends into position.

11 Finally, use twists of green paper ribbon to fill the flowerpot, so that you conceal the florist's clay and the roughly cut burlap around the inner rim.

HOLLY AND IVY
CENTERPIECE

HOLLY AND IVY *have been partnered in Christmas decorations for centuries. This gently rounded centerpiece rings the changes by using variegated ivy for extra contrast and also makes use of the ivy's berries. Artificial red berries are used to boost whatever the holly has to offer and some small evergreen leaves have been sprayed gold to introduce a touch of glamor and light to the color scheme. Presoaked oasis forms the base of the arrangement and means that the centerpiece should easily last for 10 days or so if you check it regularly and top it off with water from time to time.*

MATERIALS

4½ in. (12 cm) square of thick card
5 in. (12.5 cm) square of plastic, cut from a bin liner
All-purpose glue
Sticky tape
4½ in. (12 cm) square of presoaked oasis, 3 in. (7.5 cm) deep
12 sprigs dark green holly

12 sprigs dark green ivy with berries
12 sprigs variegated ivy
6 sprigs small evergreen leaves, sprayed gold
6 sprigs large red artificial berries
6 sprigs small red artificial berries

Opposite: Sprays of artificial berries add splashes of color to a centerpiece of variegated ivy, holly, and gold-sprayed evergreens.

1 Cover one side of the square of card with a thin layer of glue, and place the plastic square on top to make a waterproof base for the arrangement.

2 Turn the base over and fold over the edges of the plastic covering onto the card. Secure firmly along all four sides with strips of sticky tape.

3 Stand the square of presoaked oasis on the plastic-covered base. Take sprigs of holly and each type of ivy and push them into the top of the oasis, positioning them randomly.

4 Continue until the top of the oasis block is evenly covered in greenery. You will need about 3 sprigs of holly and 3 of each type of ivy to cover the oasis completely.

5 Start to add sprigs of holly and ivy to the sides of the block, aiming to use approximately the same number of sprigs of foliage for each side.

6 Continue adding foliage until the entire oasis block is evenly covered in greenery. Turn the arrangement as you work so that you can check that each side looks balanced and rounded.

7 Space the gold leaves around the arrangement. Perfect symmetry is impossible as the sprigs are all slightly different in shape and size: instead, aim for random splashes of sparkling gold.

8 Add the artificial red berries to the arrangement in the same way for a final touch of color. Check the centerpiece daily and top off the oasis with water as necessary.

IVY PLACE CARDS

THESE SIMPLE *yet elegant place cards use a combination of festive scarlet and gold to direct guests to their seats. It's a good idea to practise your handwriting first until you are satisfied with the final effect before creating the finished place cards.*

1 Cut out the place cards from thin card, to twice the depth of the finished card. Score horizontally through the middle on the top surface and fold the card in half. Write the name in the bottom right-hand corner.

MATERIALS

Scissors
Scalpel
Ruler
Thin card
Calligraphy pen
Fine gold marker pen
Ivy leaves
Gold glitter pen
Sealing wax
Matches
A decorative coin

2 Gild the ivy leaves with a gold glitter pen. Draw a gold margin around each place card using the gold marker pen, working either freehand or with a ruler.

3 Position the ivy leaf on the place card. Light the sealing wax and drip a pea-sized blob onto the leaf stalk. Press the warm wax immediately with the coin to create the effect of an old-fashioned seal.

APPLIQUÉ CLOTH AND NAPKINS

A CRISP DAMASK *cloth and set of napkins appliquéd with poinsettias, roses, and pinecones are bound to become annual favorites. To make them you'll need a sewing machine with a zigzag stitch facility to sew on the motifs and, at the same time, stop them from fraying. Before you begin, test the fabric that you have chosen to appliqué – if it's not colorfast it will spoil the tablecloth. To help you decide where to position the motifs, lay the cloth on the table and then tack round the actual tabletop. The motifs should form a border just below the table's edge.*

MATERIALS

Damask tablecloth and napkins
Printed Christmas fabric
Needle
Matching thread
Sewing machine
Scissors

Opposite: A tablecloth garlanded with appliquéd Christmas foliage and complemented by a set of matching appliquéd napkins.

MAKING THE CLOTH

1 Cut out your chosen motifs from Christmas fabric. Make sure you select a design with large motifs; small designs are difficult to work with and lack impact.

2 Lay the cloth out flat and mark the center of each side. Pin on the motifs, using the tacking stitches as a guide. Space the motifs evenly and symmetrically around the cloth.

3 Tack each motif in place, taking care to run your stitches at least ½ in. (1 cm) in from the raw edge. Remove all pins before you start using the sewing machine.

4 Zigzag stitch round the edge of each motif. Choose a thread color that matches the motifs and contrasts with the tablecloth to give a crisp edge to the appliqué work.

MAKING THE NAPKINS

1 To make the napkins, carefully cut out a motif large enough to fit comfortably in one corner when the napkin is folded. In this example, two contrasting pieces have been selected.

2 Cut out enough motifs for all the napkins, making sure they are identical. If you are using two pieces, you may need to try several combinations before you find a satisfactory arrangement.

3 Pin the completed design to one corner of the napkin and tack to hold the motif firmly in place, running the tacking stitches about ½ in. (1 cm) in from the edge.

4 Use the sewing machine to zigzag stitch round the edge of the motif in exactly the same way as you did for the tablecloth, then trim off any loose ends of thread.

QUILTED MATS AND RUNNER

Red AND GREEN *make a striking seasonal color scheme in these handsome placemats. Printed Christmas ribbon has been used to make the borders and the quilted effect comes from lining the mats with interfacing, which will also protect the table.*

MATERIALS

Thread; Needle; Scissors; Sewing machine	For the runner:
For each placemat:	*Enough fabric for two placemats (see left), plus:*
10¼ in. (26 cm) square of washable interfacing	*12¾ in. (22.5 cm) square of interfacing*
10¼ in. (26 cm) square of green cotton	*12¾ in. (22.5 cm) square of green cotton*
17¾ in. (45 cm) square of red chintz	*20¼ in. (51.5 cm) square of red chintz*
½ yd. (50 cm) of Christmas ribbon, 3 in. (7.5 cm) wide	*52 in. (132 cm) Christmas ribbon, 3 in. (7.5 cm) wide*

MAKING THE MATS

1 Place the interfacing on top of the square of green cotton. Tack neatly round the edges to join the two pieces of fabric together.

2 Lay the red chintz right side down and fold in 3⅝ in. (6.5 cm) on all four sides. Press with an iron to leave a bold crease line.

3 Open out the chintz and place cotton and interfacing inside. Turn under the raw edge by ⅝ in. (1.5 cm) to give a 3 in. (7.5 cm) border, and pin.

4 Tack along the pinned lines, keeping close to the edge and making sure that you stitch right through all three layers of fabric.

5 Lay the Christmas ribbon along one side of the red border so that an equal amount of red chintz is visible above and below the ribbon. Pin the ribbon to hold it in place.

6 Form a neat mitered corner by folding the ribbon up at a right angle and then back on itself by 45°, laying it along the adjoining side of the mat. Pin it in place.

7 When you get to the final corner, cut off the excess ribbon to align with the edge of the ribbon border on the adjoining side.

8 Fold the ribbon under at 45° to form the last mitered corner and pin it in place. Then start tacking along the inner and outer edges of the ribbon border.

9 Tack along the mitered corners, too, keeping about ¼ in. (6 mm) from the edge of the ribbon. Remove the pins as you go.

MAKING THE RUNNER

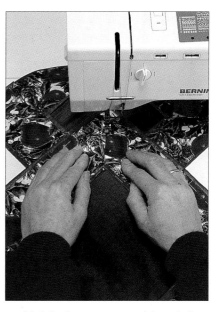

10 Machine stitch the ribbon border in place, keeping close to the edge of the ribbon. Remove tacking and press the mat with a hot iron.

1 Make up one large square and two smaller ones (see pages 82-84). Overlap the large square on the small squares in a diamond formation and tack together.

2 To join the squares, machine stitch around all edges where the large and small squares overlap and along the mitered corners of the ribbon border on the large square.

FESTIVE FOODS

A T *CHRISTMAS* *every cook knows it's worth spending a little longer in the kitchen: the difference between homemade dishes and store-bought is vast. Here are recipes for cookies, truffles, cakes and the quintessential plum pudding. Stocking up the larder with good things to eat is supremely satisfying.*

GINGERBREAD HOUSE

The elegant artifice built from gingerbread and icing is a more refined version of the homely gingerbread house made every year at Christmas. If you want it to survive the festive season, keep it out of reach of little fingers. Even if you can stop the children from playing with it, they'll almost certainly try to eat it.

INGREDIENTS

½ cup butter
Generous ½ cup molasses
½ cup honey
3 cups all-purpose flour
1 cup ground almonds
½ tablespoon ground ginger
1 teaspoon mixed spice
½ teaspoon nutmeg
2 teaspoons baking soda
Scant ½ cup preserved ginger, chopped
Scant ½ cup mixed peel, chopped
A little milk
Cooking oil

Note: you will need three times the above quantities to make the house pictured right.
For the icing:
3 cups confectioner's sugar
Whites of 2 large eggs
1 teaspoon lemon juice

You will also need:
A rolling pin
2 baking trays
Card and tracing paper
Small kitchen knife
Pastry bag and tips
9 x 13 in. (23 x 33 cm) cakeboard

1 Using tracing paper, copy the template on page 146 onto the card. Warm the butter, molasses and honey in a pan until blended. Cool slightly. Mix the dry ingredients, chopped ginger and peel in a bowl. Add the cooled butter mixture and stir together. Turn out onto a floured surface and knead lightly, adding a little milk if dough is too dry, flour if too wet. Roll out onto the oiled baking tray to a depth of ½ in. (1 cm).

2 Lay the template on the dough and cut around it. Bake for 20 minutes in a preheated oven at 400°F until brown. Cool before removing from tray. If the gingerbread has spread, replace template and cut out again. Repeat the process for the sides and roof pieces using the templates on page 147. To make the back, use the front template for size, but don't cut out windows and door.

3 Beat egg whites until frothy. Slowly add sifted sugar and lemon juice, beating until peaks are formed. Fill the pastry bag and use a small tip to pipe around windows and door. Pipe a double line around the front and fill in with dots. Pipe a border of dots and stars along the bottom. Decorate the sides as shown.

4 Pipe a criss-crossed border along the top edge of the roof pieces and a lattice on the main section. Pipe a dot into each diamond on the lattice. There is no need to decorate the back of the house, as it won't be visible.

5 Reserve a little icing and beat the remaining icing until it becomes much thicker. Fill the pastry bag and insert a larger tip. Pipe a generous line of icing along the side and back of the cakeboard and pipe another line along the side of the back wall where it will meet the side wall. Stand the back and one side wall on the lines of icing and push the side against the back.

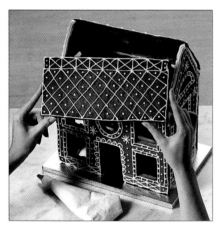

6 Add the other side and the front of the house in the same manner. The icing "glue" is very strong and should hold the pieces firmly when set. Pipe along the top edge of the front and the gable end, then press the front section of the roof gently into place. Attach the back of the roof in the same way.

7 When the two roof sections are in place, there will be a small gap at the top. Pipe along both edges and fix the roof ridge in place.

8 Use the kitchen knife to clean away any icing glue that oozes out of the joins and from under the base. Using the smallest tip and the original icing, pipe over the joins to disguise them.

GINGERBREAD MEN

INGREDIENTS

1²/₃ cups all-purpose flour
2 teaspoons baking powder
1-2 teaspoons ground ginger
¹/₃ cup butter
Generous ¹/₃ cup superfine sugar
4 tablespoons molasses
2-4 tablespoons milk
Cooking oil

Sift the flour with the baking powder and ground ginger. Rub in the butter until the mixture resembles fine breadcrumbs.

Mix in the sugar, warmed molasses and milk. Knead until smooth and roll out to ¹/₄ in. (6 mm) thick. Cut out men with a cutter and transfer to an oiled baking sheet.

Leave to rest in a refrigerator for 20-30 minutes, then bake in a preheated oven at 375°F for 10-12 minutes. Cool the gingerbread men on a rack.

Makes about 8 cookies.

CHRISTMAS SUGAR COOKIES

Children always enjoy stamping out cookies with cutters and you can let them exercise their artistic talents when it comes to decorating them.

INGREDIENTS

2 cups all-purpose flour
¼ teaspoon salt
¾ cup salted butter, softened
¾ cup superfine sugar
1 large egg
1 teaspoon pure vanilla extract
Colored sugars or other decorations

Preheat the oven to 325°F. In a medium bowl combine the flour and salt with a wire whisk. In a large mixing bowl cream the butter and sugar with an electric mixer on medium speed. Add the egg and vanilla, and beat until well mixed.

Scrape down sides of bowl, then add the flour mixture. Blend on low speed until just combined – be careful not to overmix.

Gather dough into a ball. Flatten the ball into a disk, wrap tightly in plastic wrap and chill for 1 hour.

On a floured surface, roll out dough to ¼ in. (6 mm) thick. Cut dough into shapes with cookie cutters and place on ungreased cookie sheets. Decorate with colored sugars and bake for 13-15 minutes, without letting them brown. Transfer cookies with a spatula to a cool, flat surface.
Makes 3 dozen cookies.

CHOCOLATE PRALINES

These classic chocolate pralines are a delicious after-dinner treat and would also make a much-appreciated present. Using a good quality chocolate makes all the difference to the finished recipe.

INGREDIENTS

Scant 2½ cups superfine sugar
Lemon juice
Scant 2½ cups whole hazelnuts, skinned
1 cup whole blanched almonds
Cooking oil
3½ squares good-quality dark chocolate, melted

Melt the sugar in a saucepan with a few drops of lemon juice. Warm the nuts gently in the oven before mixing with the sugar and heating until they are a rich golden brown color. Pour the mixture on to a well-oiled baking tray and leave to cool and set.

Break up the praline and process it to a fine paste, then gradually add the melted chocolate, keeping a little back.

Shape the mixture into balls and dip in the remaining melted chocolate. Leave to harden.
Makes 2¼ pounds.

SUGARED NUTS

Sweet and spicy pecans or walnuts are traditionally served with dessert but make an irresistible appetizer.

INGREDIENTS

1 egg white
2 cups pecan or walnut halves
½ cup sugar
½ teaspoon salt
½ teaspoon cinnamon

Preheat the oven to 225°F. Beat the egg white with 1 tablespoon water, and dip the nuts into it. Roll them in the mixed sugar, salt and cinnamon.

Spread on a cookie sheet, and then bake for 1 hour, stirring the nuts every 15 minutes. Cool, then store in the refrigerator.
Makes about 2 cups.

BRANDY SNAPS

These pretty lacy cookies can be slightly tricky to shape but, once you've made a few, it gets easier and easier.

INGREDIENTS

¼ cup butter, softened

Scant ⅔ cup superfine sugar

¼ cup corn syrup

⅓ cup all-purpose flour

¼ teaspoon ground ginger

Cooking oil

Cream the butter and sugar together until light and fluffy. Beat in the syrup, then fold in the flour and ginger.

Shape the mixture into walnut-sized pieces and press just two or three pieces onto a well-oiled baking sheet, keeping them well apart, as the mixture will spread as they cook. Bake at 325°F for 5-8 minutes until golden-colored.

Remove the brandy snaps from the oven and cool very slightly. Then lift each one carefully with a knife blade and shape it around the handle of an oiled wooden spoon. Leave the brandy snap to cool for a minute or so before removing from the spoon.

Makes about 8 brandy snaps.

CHOCOLATE TRUFFLES

Truffles are a rich finishing touch to a meal – perfect served with after-dinner coffee.

INGREDIENTS

6 oz. dark chocolate
2 tablespoons almond-flavored liqueur
(amaretto) or orange-flavored liqueur
3 tablespoons sweet butter
½ cup confectioner's sugar
½ cup ground almonds
1 ¾ oz. grated chocolate
Paper candy wrappers

Melt the dark chocolate using a double boiler and stir in your chosen liqueur.

Then stir in the butter until melted. Add the confectioner's sugar and the ground almonds and stir to combine smoothly.

Chill the mixture until solid enough to handle, then break into about 24 pieces and roll them into small balls.

Spread the grated chocolate on a plate and roll the truffles in it until coated. Put each truffle in an individual paper wrapper and store in the refrigerator. They will keep for about 2 weeks.

To vary the mixture, use milk chocolate instead, and finish the truffles by dipping them in melted chocolate.
Makes about 24 truffles.

CRANBERRY RELISH

An incredibly simple homemade relish that tastes far better than anything store-bought. Serve it with hot or cold meats.

INGREDIENTS

2 cups cranberries
1 small orange
¾ cup sugar

Wash and drain the cranberries. Cut up the orange and remove the seeds, but do not peel. Chop the cranberries and orange coarsely with a food chopper or in a food processor; add the sugar and stir well. Let the mixture stand for at least 30 minutes before serving. *Serves 6.*

MINCE PIES

Serve them to friends, carolers, and anyone who visits over the holiday, but don't forget to leave one out for Santa Claus on Christmas Eve.

INGREDIENTS

For 2 pounds of mincemeat
8 oz. cooking apples, peeled, cored and chopped
¹⁄₃ cup dried figs, chopped
¾ cup muscatel raisins
²⁄₃ cup golden raisins
¾ cup currants
¹⁄₃ cup mixed candied peel, chopped
¹⁄₃ cup whole blanched almonds, chopped
¾ cup soft dark brown sugar
Grated rind and juice of half a lemon
¹⁄₂ teaspoon ground cinnamon
Large pinch ground nutmeg
¹⁄₂ teaspoon ground ginger
Large pinch ground cloves
2 oz. suet (optional)
¹⁄₄ cup of brandy

For the pastry:
1 ²⁄₃ cups all-purpose flour
¹⁄₂ cup butter
1 tablespoon superfine sugar
2 egg yolks
A little milk
Superfine sugar

To make the mincemeat, put the apples, dried fruit, and candied peel through a mincer or food processor. Add the other ingredients and mix well. Spoon into sterilized jars and press down well to exclude any air. Seal the jars and store in a cool, dry place for one month for the flavors to develop.

To make the mince pies, rub the butter gently into the flour. Add the sugar and egg yolks and a little cold water and mix to a stiff dough.

Wrap the dough in plastic wrap and chill until ready to use. Roll it out ¼ in. (6 mm) thick and using 3 in. (7.5 cm) pastry cutters, cut out about 20 round bases. Cut out another 20, slightly smaller, rounds to make the lids.

Press the bases into muffin pans and spoon in the mincemeat. Brush water round the edges of the bases and seal on the pastry lids.

Brush lids lightly with a little milk and make a small hole in each with a skewer. Bake at 400°F for 25-30 minutes. Dredge the tops with superfine sugar and serve them hot or cold.
Makes about 20 pies.

LIGHT FRUIT CAKE

You can use any combination of candied fruits and nuts for this cake, but stuffed dates are particularly good. Make them yourself by filling each date with a nut and then rolling it in sugar.

INGREDIENTS

1 cup butter
2 cups sugar
1 tablespoon pure vanilla extract
7 eggs, separated
2¼ cups flour
1 teaspoon salt
2 teaspoons baking powder
1 cup milk
2 cups seedless white raisins
2 cups pecans in large pieces
1 cup candied cherries
1 cup candied pineapple in large pieces
2 cups dates, stuffed with nuts and rolled in sugar

Preheat the oven to 325°F. Butter and lightly flour two 5 x 9 in. (12.5 x 22 cm) loaf pans.

Cream the butter and slowly beat in the sugar until light. Add the vanilla and the egg yolks and beat well. Mix the flour, salt, and baking powder, and stir them and ½ cup of the milk into the mixture.

Add the remaining milk and beat well. Stir in the raisins and pecans.

Beat the egg whites separately until they are stiff but not dry. Gently stir a third of the whites into the batter, then fold in the remaining whites carefully.

Spoon a layer of batter into each pan. Arrange rows of candied cherries and pineapple and the dates on top, then cover with the remaining batter, filling each pan one-half to two-thirds full. Bake for about 1 hour or until a toothpick comes out clean. Cool in the pans for 5 minutes before turning the cakes out onto racks. When completely cool, wrap well and store in an airtight container for up to two months.
Makes 2 loaves.

PLUM PUDDING

The traditional Christmas pudding needs no introduction. If you have the nerve – and a steady hand – carry it to the table flaming with warmed rum.

INGREDIENTS

3 slices white bread, torn into pieces
⅔ cup evaporated milk
⅔ cup ground beef suet or shortening
⅔ cup packed brown sugar
1 beaten egg
1 teaspoon finely shredded orange peel
¼ cup orange juice or rum
1½ cups raisins
¾ cup snipped pitted whole dates
½ cup diced candied fruits and peels
⅓ cup chopped walnuts
¾ cup all-purpose flour
1½ teaspoons ground cinnamon
¾ teaspoon baking soda
½ teaspoon ground cloves
½ teaspoon ground mace or nutmeg
¼ cup rum (optional)

Soak the bread in the evaporated milk for a few minutes until it is softened. Beat it lightly to break it up. Stir in the suet or shortening, brown sugar, egg, orange peel, and the orange juice. Then add the raisins, dates, fruits and peels, and the nuts.

Mix together the flour, cinnamon, baking soda, cloves and mace, and add to the fruit mixture, stirring until combined. Transfer mixture to a well-greased mold or pudding basin and cover with foil, pressing it tightly against the rim of the mold.

Place the mold on a rack in a deep pan and add 1 in. (2.5 cm) boiling water. Cover and bring to a gentle boil. Steam the pudding for 2½ to 3 hours or until a toothpick inserted near the center comes out clean, adding more boiling water if necessary.

Cool for 10 minutes before removing from the mold, and serve immediately. Heat rum, if using, until hot; ignite with a match and pour over pudding.

Or wrap and store the pudding in the refrigerator for up to 2 weeks. To reheat, wrap it in foil and place on a baking sheet. Bake at 350°F for 30 to 40 minutes until the pudding is hot.

Serves 8-10.

BRANDY BUTTER

The perfect accompaniment to plum pudding tastes equally good spread on hot mince pies.

INGREDIENTS

¾ cup unsalted butter, softened

¼ teaspoon ground nutmeg

¼ teaspoon grated lemon zest

3 cups confectioner's sugar (sifted)

2-3 tablespoons brandy

Beat the butter until soft, then beat in the nutmeg and lemon zest.

Gradually add the sugar with the brandy, beating well after each addition.

Mound the brandy butter into small dishes or roll it into walnut-sized balls.

Serves 6-8.

HOT SPICED CIDER

Make this warming drink with hard cider if you want to get celebrations off to a flying start, or use apple juice in more sober circumstances.

INGREDIENTS

8 cups hard apple cider or apple juice
¼ - ½ cup packed brown sugar
6 in. (15 cm) stick cinnamon
1 teaspoon whole allspice
1 teaspoon whole cloves
8 thin orange wedges or slices (optional)
8 whole cloves (optional)

Combine the apple cider or juice and brown sugar in a large saucepan. Place the cinnamon, allspice, and cloves in a double layer of cheesecloth, bring up the corners, and tie together. Add spice bag to cider mixture. Bring to a boil, then reduce heat, cover, and simmer for at least 10 minutes. Stud orange wedges or slices with cloves, if using. Discard spice bag and serve cider with studded orange wedges or slices.
Makes about eight 8 oz. servings.

RUM PUNCH

Watch out: this deceptively fruity punch has hidden depths.

INGREDIENTS

1 bottle (750 ml) light rum
1 can (46 oz.) pineapple juice, chilled
½ can (6 oz.) frozen orange juice concentrate, defrosted and undiluted
4 cups grapefruit juice, chilled
1 cup grenadine syrup
1½ cups apricot brandy
Ice mold or ice chunk

Mix the rum, pineapple, orange, and grapefruit juice, grenadine syrup and brandy in a large punch bowl. Add the ice mold or chunk.
Makes twenty 6 oz. servings.

EGGNOG

With plenty of nourishing ingredients in it, you can kid yourself that eggnog is actually doing you good as you drink it. Leave out the alcohol and top off with more milk (see right) and it's a good way of persuading children to drink their daily ration.

INGREDIENTS

6 beaten eggs
2 cups milk
⅓ cup sugar
2-4 tablespoons light rum
2-4 tablespoons bourbon
1 teaspoon vanilla
1 cup whipping cream
2 tablespoons sugar
Ground nutmeg

In a large heavy saucepan mix the eggs, milk and sugar. Cook and stir over medium heat until mixture coats the back of a metal spoon.

Remove from heat and cool pan in a sink or bowl of ice water while stirring for 1 to 2 minutes. Stir in rum, bourbon and vanilla, and chill anywhere from 4-24 hours.

To serve, whip cream and sugar till soft peaks form. Transfer chilled egg mixture to a punch bowl and fold in the whipped cream. Serve at once, sprinkled with nutmeg.
Makes about ten 4 oz. servings.

CHOCOLATE EGGNOG
Prepare as above except stir ¼ to ⅓ cup chocolate-flavored syrup into the egg mixture before chilling.

NONALCOHOLIC EGGNOG
Prepare as above, except omit rum and bourbon. Increase milk to 2¼ - 2½ cups.

GIFTS TO MAKE

HOMEMADE PRESENTS *are extra special. The time and effort that go into creating them make them real labors of love. Here are some gift ideas for both adults and children, ranging from the simplest lavender sachets to a more challenging traditional rag doll and an intricate cross-stitch sampler to work.*

LAVENDER SACHETS

T INY SACHETS *filled with lavender or potpourri make ideal tokens of affection for friends at Christmas. Make square versions to scent a drawer and little gathered bags on ribbon loops to hang in the closet. Using sheer ribbon to make the bags cuts down on sewing and allows the lavender or potpourri to show through prettily. Because of the sachet's size, if you decide to use potpourri, make sure you use a fine-textured mixture. Trim the lavender bags with braid and a ribbon rose for a finishing touch.*

1 To make a gathered sachet, fold the sheer ribbon across the width and overcast the sides. Neaten the top and fill with lavender or fine potpourri.

2 Run a line of gathering just below the top and draw up tightly. Trim with a ready-made miniature tassel.

3 To make a flat drawer sachet, fold the sheer ribbon across the width and overcast the top and bottom.

4 Fill the resulting pocket with lavender and overcast the final top edges together. Sew lace or decorative braid all around, gathering it at the corners for extra fullness.

5 To hang the sachet, make a loop from narrow ribbon and stitch it to one corner. Trim sachet with a ribbon rose (see instructions on page 141).

see instructions on page 141

MATERIALS

Needle; Thread; Scissors

For the gathered bag sachet:
*7 in. (18 cm) of sheer ribbon,
2¼ in. (56 mm) wide
Dried lavender or fine potpourri
Ready-made small tassel for trimming*

For the drawer sachet:
*7 in. (18 cm) of sheer ribbon, 2¼ in.
(56 mm) wide
Dried lavender or fine potpourri
12 in. (30 cm) of lace or decorative braid,
⅜ in. (9 mm) wide
10½ in. (26 cm) of ribbon, ¼ in. (6 mm) wide for
ribbon rose
8 in. (20 cm) of satin ribbon, 1/16 in. (1.5 mm) wide,
for hanging loop*

PUFF DOLL

A DEMURE LITTLE *doll to enchant young and old alike. She would be equally at home in a little girl's toy box or on a not-so-little girl's dressing table. The doll is made from puffs of fabric – an old English country craft – and so doesn't have a stuffed body like conventional rag dolls. Choose a tiny floral print to make her dress – fabric with a large pattern would be too overwhelming on this scale. When stitching the fabric, make your seams ¹/₄ in. (6 mm) wide, but when working in felt for the head, hands, and feet, join the pieces together by overcasting neatly.*

....

MATERIALS

Needle; Scissors; Pins
14 x 36 in. (35 x 90 cm) piece of medium-weight cotton-blend floral print dress fabric
Matching thread, plus black thread
14 x 36 in. (35 x 90 cm) piece of medium-weight cotton-blend white fabric; Tracing paper
4¾ x 8 in. (12 x 20 cm) piece of cream-colored felt
Washable polyester batting
3 x 4 in. (7.5 x 10 cm) piece of black felt
Scrap of stiff card

1½ yd. (1.4 m) of narrow, round elastic
24 in. (60 cm) of eyelet embroidery, 1 in (2.5 cm) wide
36 in. (90 cm) of black lace, ⅜ in. (9 mm) wide
Stranded embroidery yarn or fine knitting yarn
Brown domed sequins, about ³/₁₆ in. (5 mm) diameter
Pink-red stranded embroidery floss
Heavyweight sew-in interfacing; Fusible interfacing
Clear adhesive; 18 in. (45 cm) of narrow braid
6 in. (15 cm) of satin ribbon, ¹/₄ in. (6 mm) wide

Opposite: This pretty rag doll is perfect in every way, from her lace-trimmed bonnet to her black felt shoes.

1 To make each puff, use a pair of compasses to draw a circle to the required size (see step 2) on the fabric. Cut it out and fold into four, then snip off the very tip of the folded corner. Open up the circle and gather all round with running stitches, close to the raw edge. Draw up the stitches, with the right side of the fabric outermost. Flatten the puff, raw edges in the middle, before fastening off the threads.

2 Make up the following puffs. In floral fabric: 6 circles 4 in. (10 cm) in diameter (A); 8 circles 3 in. (7.5 cm) in diameter (B); 12 circles 2¼ in. (6 cm) in diameter (C). In white fabric: 2 circles 5½ in. (13 cm) diameter (D); 1 circle 4¾ in. (12 cm) in diameter (E); 1 circle 4 in. (10 cm) in diameter (F); 24 circles 3 in. (7.5 cm) in diameter (G).

3 Trace the pattern pieces on page 148 and use them to cut 1 face and 3 back head pieces from cream felt. Join 2 back head pieces between A-B and join the third piece in the same way but leave it open between the notches. Join the head to each side of the face. Turn right side out and stuff very firmly, then close the seam.

4 Cut 4 hands from cream felt. For each hand overcast two pieces together, leaving the straight edge open. Turn right side out and stuff. Gather round the top edge, then overcast.

5 Cut 2 shoes and 2 soles from black felt. For each foot, join the front of the shoe between C-D; then fit the lower edge round the sole, matching the notches (E) with the seam at center front and back. Overcast together and turn right side out. Cut out the sole again, slightly smaller, in card and fit inside the shoe. Stuff the feet and gather round the top edge before overcasting.

6 To assemble the doll, cut a piece of elastic 18 in. (45 cm) long and mark the center with a pin. Measure 2¾ in. (7 cm) each side of the pin. Fold the elastic and push the loops through the center of 4 B floral puffs and 6 C puffs. Sew a hand to the elastic.

Left: Measure and mark the elastic, then thread on the sleeve puffs before sewing on the hands.

Above: Sew the center of body elastic under the head. Thread all four lengths through the body puffs.

Left: Sew elastic to feet and add puffs.

7 Sew the center of an 8 in. (20 cm) length of elastic underneath the head. Push the cut ends (c) through 2 A floral puffs. Slip the arms' elastic between the two head elastics. Take all four ends down through the remaining 4 A floral puffs and the single white puff F.

8 Sew the center of a 12 in. (30 cm) length of elastic to the top of a shoe. Thread the cut ends (d) through 12 white G puffs to make a leg. Make the other leg in the same way.

9 Push all four ends (d) through the 2 white D puffs and E puff. Space the puffs out evenly, then knot all the ends together (b to d, b to d, c to d, and c to d). Sew each knot to keep it from slipping.

10 To make the petticoat, cut a piece of white fabric 4⅜ in. (11 cm) deep x 14 in. (35 cm) wide and join the short edges. Trim the bottom edge with eyelet embroidery. Gather the top, fit the petticoat on the doll, and draw up the gathers round the elastic beneath the lowest floral puff.

11 To make the skirt, cut a piece of floral fabric 5½ x 16 in. (13 x 40 cm) and join the short edges. Turn up and stitch a ½ in. (1 cm) hem and trim with black lace. Gather the top edge and fit onto the doll, over her petticoat.

12 Take a thread up through the top of the skirt and through the body puffs – close to the center front – then back again, tacking them down.

13 To make the hair, separate three 30 in. (75 cm) strands of yarn, then put them together again and fold into four. Stitch the middle of the bunch to the center of the forehead, then take the ends smoothly down over each side of the face and round to the back, and sew in place.

14 Repeat until the head is almost covered. When the uncovered area is quite small, you may need to fold the yarn into six and then eight.

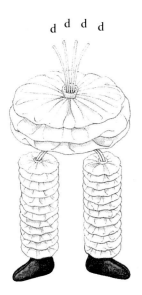

Left: Thread all four leg elastics up through the lower body puffs.

15 Sew the eye sequins (dome side out) to the face with black thread. Then work short straight stitches for the eyebrows and nose. Embroider a V-shape with three strands of pink-red floss for the mouth.

16 Gather an 8 in. (20 cm) length of lace for the collar. Gather two 6 in. (15 cm) pieces for cuffs. Cut the bonnet brim and back from heavyweight interfacing. Using fusible interfacing, bond floral fabric to both sides. Place the straight edge of the brim to the bonnet back, matching the two points F and the notch, and overcast. Glue braid over the stitches and round the brim.

17 Gather an 8 in. (20 cm) length of eyelet embroidery and pin it evenly over the top of the head; draw up and adjust the gathers, then sew in place.

18 Make a tiny bow near the center of the ribbon. Sew the ends to the sides of the head so that the bow is under the chin. Finally, sew the bonnet into place.

TOY SOLDIERS

THESE TRADITIONAL *toy soldiers are made mostly from paper. They are ideal gifts for children and would look charming peeking out of the top of a stocking on Christmas morning. From the cockades on their helmets to the buttons on their red felt jackets, the soldiers are complete down to the smallest detail. Turn them into a marching band and give them small Christmas tree decorations in the shape of musical instruments to hold. Or, if you prefer, you can follow the instructions given and kit them out with a paper drum and a band-leader's baton.*

MATERIALS

*3 sheets of medium-weight white paper,
each 8¼ x 11½ in. (21 x 29 cm)
Black felt-tip pen; Clear adhesive
8½ in. (22 cm) length of blue ribbon, ¼ in. (6 mm) wide
Sheets of good quality scrap paper (from old magazines, etc)
Thin card; Scissors
6 in. (15 cm) square of red felt; Tracing paper
2⅜ x 3 in. (6 x 7.5 cm) piece of white felt
4⅜ in. (11 cm) length of gold braid; Needle
2 tiny red beads; Red and white sewing threads*

*4⅜ x 6 in. (11 x 15 cm) piece of black felt
Scraps of pink, black and brown paper
Gold gift tie, ¼ in. (6 mm) wide
6 in. (15 cm) length of black ribbon, ¼ in. (6 mm) wide
Assorted gold sequins
8 in. (20 cm) length of white ribbon, ¼ in. (6 mm) wide
30 in. (75 cm) length of white ribbon, ¹⁄₁₆ in. (1.5 mm) wide
Colored paper, thin cord, tooth picks, a thin skewer and a
bead, to finish*

Opposite: A parade of three sprightly paper-and-felt toy soldiers is sure to appeal to little boys.

1 Lay a sheet of white paper horizontally and, from the left, mark off 5 in. (12.5 cm). Write "overlap" on the righthand area. On the left, mark a short horizontal line across, 1⅜ in. (3.5 cm) from the top edge to indicate the position of the hair and helmet. In black pen, mark a central vertical line 2¾ in. (7 cm) up from the bottom edge for the legs.

2 Pencil in vertical lines 1¼ in. (3 cm) away to each side. Then cut and glue 4¼ in. (11 cm) lengths of blue ribbon onto the lines for the trouser stripes.

3 Beginning at the righthand edge, roll up the paper into a tube 1⅝ in. (4 cm) in diameter and glue the overlap. Roll up the other two sheets of white paper and fit them inside, allowing them to open out to fit snugly. Use sheets of waste paper cut to size, to fill up the inside.

4 To make the jacket, cut a piece of red felt 2¾ in. deep by 5½ in. wide (7 x 14 cm). Mark the arm positions 1⅜ in. (3.5 cm) in from the sides and ⅜ in. (9 mm) down from the jacket's top edge.

5 Using the pattern on page 146, trace 2 arms onto thin card and cut them out. Glue red felt to both sides up to the broken line. Cover the hands to the broken line with white felt gloves. Glue gold braid on to the top edge of the arm to form the epaulettes.

6 Sew the arms to each side of the jacket by passing the needle through the arm, then through a red bead, then into the jacket at the placement mark. By working the needle back and forth, you can make sure the arm is secure yet still moves easily.

7 Using the pattern, cut the helmet top from card and glue it to the black felt. Cut V-shaped notches on the edges to form tabs. Place the helmet top on top of the tube and glue the tabs to hold it in place. Cut a piece of black felt 1½ in. deep by 5½ in. wide (3.7 x 14 cm) for the helmet.

8 Cut the face from a scrap of pink paper and the helmet peak from black paper. Glue the peak to the face as marked, then draw in the features using a black pen.

9 Glue the face to the tube, with the top level with the marked horizontal line. Cut a 1¼ in. (3 cm) deep strip of brown paper and glue it round the tube for hair, cutting it so that it overlaps the face.

10 Glue the black felt helmet strip round the tube, overlapping the face as indicated by the broken line on the pattern. Overlap the edges at the back.

11 Glue the jacket around the tube, overlapping the face as indicated by the broken line. Use gold gift tie to make a collar for the jacket and make a belt from black ribbon. Use sequins for buttons. Arrange the wide white ribbon over the shoulder and across the body, gluing it at the side.

12 Trim the helmet by gluing gift tie around the bottom. To make a cockade, cut 10 pieces of very narrow white ribbon 2¾ in. (7 cm) long and bind together tightly at the center, then fold in half and bind tightly again, close to the original stitching at the center of the fold, before you glue them to the helmet. Glue narrow braid around the face.

13 Cut out a ¾ in. (2 cm) diameter circle of black felt and halve it for the feet. Glue them to the base at each side of the vertical leg line.

14 Make a drum by cutting several 1 x 12 in. (2.5 x 30 cm) lengths of paper. Roll one up and glue to form a ring about 2 in. (5 cm) in diameter. Roll up the remaining strips and fit them inside. Cut two 2⅜ in. (6 cm) diameter circles of thin card and glue one to each side of the ring. Cut a 1⅜ x 8 in. (3.5 x 20 cm) strip of colored paper and glue it round the outside. Trim with gift tie ribbon and fix thin cord through the top edges to hang around the soldier's neck. Add toothpicks for drumsticks, gluing them to the soldier's hands. To make the bandleader's baton, glue a bead to the tip of a 5½ in. (14 cm) wooden skewer.

FLAVORED OILS

INFUSING OILS *or vinegars with herbs and spices turns them into attractive gifts for friends and family, especially if you present them in pretty bottles. Herbs, chilies and slices of citrus fruits used to flavor the oils and vinegars are not only delicious but also have the added bonus of looking decorative, too. A bland oil such as sunflower will accept the added flavors most readily; if using vinegar, be sure to choose a good quality one. Any bottle or wide-necked jar can be used to hold the infusion. The most important thing to remember is to sterilize the containers before you fill them, and then to seal them properly afterward.*

MATERIALS

Freshly picked herbs
Dried whole spices
Citrus fruits
Whole red chilies
Clear glass bottles of various shapes and sizes
Oil
Vinegar (malt or rice)

1 Choose herbs and spices from the combinations listed below. Wash the herbs thoroughly and dry on paper towels. Buy freshly dried spices - don't make do with old ones from the back of a cupboard, they won't be as flavorful.

2 Put the flavorings into bottles and add enough oil or vinegar to cover all the ingredients completely. Seal the bottles and leave for two weeks in a cool dark cupboard. Try the following: **Chili Oil**, red chilies, black peppercorns and sunflower oil; **Orange Oil**, orange peel on a wooden skewer with coriander seeds and sunflower oil; **Lemon Oil**, lemon slices, bay leaves, black peppercorns and sunflower oil; **Garlic Oil**, cloves of garlic on wooden skewers in olive oil; **Coriander Vinegar**, sprigs of fresh coriander and vinegar.

Above: Cutting citrus peel into spirals looks good as well as being easier to feed into a narrow-necked bottle.

Left: Skewering garlic cloves and bay leaves is a neat way of presenting the flavorings, while rosemary sprigs are the perfect partner for olive oil.

CHRISTMAS SAMPLER

ANTIQUE SAMPLERS *are highly prized today. Stitch your own Christmas version and you could be creating a valuable family heirloom, as well as following a centuries-old tradition.*

....

You can use the seasonal motifs in this sampler, enlarged in more detail on the page overleaf, to design your own. Use two strands of stranded embroidery cotton for the cross-stitch, and one strand for the backstitch outlines. The gold and silver embroidery is worked with three strands. Match your thread colors to the pictured sampler and follow the hints below.

Letters and Numbers Use these to make up a Christmas message or a name. The single diagonal stitches in the decorative motif on the capital letters are worked in gold or silver. Dot the "i" and "j" in the lower case alphabet with French knots.

Front Door Make long stitches across the pale blue fanlight to divide it into panes, couching them down with a single strand. Outline the door frame and tubs with dark brown, the inner panels with mid-brown.

Snowman Outline the snow with dark blue. Use four strands of black thread together and work straight stitches over two blocks for the hat brim.

Santa Claus Outline the sack and presents, the hands and fur trimming with black, and also backstitch the inner sides of sleeves. Use two strands of black for eyes.

Pudding Outline the top and plate with mid-brown.

Christmas Rose Outline the cream petals with brown.

Silver Bells Outline these with dark grey.

Robin Use two strands and work in straight stitches for the beak and leg, but use only one strand for the feet.

Stockings Outline these with black.

Candlestick Outline the stand with a darker shade, and the candle glow with orange.

Lantern Shade outward from bright yellow to deep orange, then divide the panes with a single strand of black. Use a single strand of green for the sprigs of fir.

Cracker Outline with the darkest shade.

Glass Baubles Work the sprigs of fir with a single strand of dark green.

Skating Girl Outline the bonnet, cap, skirt, petticoat and muff with darker shades of the main color. Use two strands of black and long straight stitches for the skates.

Skating Boy Outline the face and hand, hat (but not pompom), scarf, tunic, sleeve, trousers and boots with dark shades. Make a French knot for the eye.

MATERIALS

Cream Aida fabric with 16 blocks of threads to 1 in. (2.5 cm)
Stranded embroidery cotton in a wide selection of colors
Silver or gold thread
Needle
Scissors

Opposite: The seasonal images on this Christmas sampler have been worked in a mixture of cross-stitch and back-stitch, in a tradition that dates back hundreds of years.

DECORATED CANDLES

ONE OF THE quickest gifts to make are these candles, which have been artfully transformed with the use of delicate dried leaves, pine cones, and fragrant cinnamon sticks.

· ·

1 Make sure that the candles are free from dust and debris. Check that each one will stand flat without wobbling.

2 To decorate a candle with lightweight delicate items such as leaves, heat an old metal spoon over a gas flame and rub it over the surface of the candle to warm the wax.

3 Working quickly, press the leaves into the warm wax and hold them in position until the wax cools.

4 The cinnamon sticks are heavier and so must be glued to the candle. Apply a thin layer of glue to the candle and press on the cinnamon sticks, packing them together tightly.

5 To attach the pine cones, first break off the scales of the cone on one side to form a flat surface, then glue them to the base of the candle.

6 Candles with applied decoration may flare up when the flame reaches an embedded leaf, so keep an eye on them when burning. In any case, candles should never be left burning unattended. The flame should not be allowed to reach the cinnamon stick and pine cone borders or any glued-on decoration. Extinguish it before it burns too low.

MATERIALS

A selection of candles in different sizes
Rubber-based glue
Decorative items such as cinnamon sticks, dried leaves, and pine cones

---

Opposite: Simple natural decorations and kitchen spices can transform a candle into a much-appreciated gift.

CARDS AND WRAPPING

THERE'S NO *better way to personalize Christmas cards than to make your own – and the same goes for wrapping paper and even gift boxes. A few hours work is all it takes to create original designs that will intrigue and surprise family and friends.*

STRIPED
WRAPPING PAPER

TO MAKE *hand-decorated wrapping paper, use paint mixed*
with wallpaper paste, which slows down the drying time.
However, you will still need to work quickly to finish your design.

> ### MATERIALS
>
> *Fungicide-free wallpaper paste, mixed with water to a runny consistency*
> *Pale blue sketching paper*
> *Acrylic paint in purple and dark blue*
> *Two dishes for paint; Newspaper*
> *Large paintbrush*
> *Rubber decorator's combs, each about 1¼ in. (3 cm) wide,*
> *one with a flat edge and one with serrated teeth*

1 Add the paint to the wallpaper paste and pour into dishes. Lay the sketching paper on newspaper and paint three large blue stripes.

Opposite: Create your own highly original wrapping paper with paste painting, a traditional technique once used to make endpapers for books.

2 Add two thick stripes of purple paint, using large sweeping strokes and blending lightly where they join the stripes of blue paint.

3 Working quickly before the paint begins to dry, wiggle the serrated rubber comb swiftly along the overlap where the two colors meet.

4 Then wiggle the end of the flat-edged decorator's comb between the lines formed by the serrated comb, creating a wide wavy line. Leave to dry.

STENCILED WRAPPING PAPER

STENCILING *is one of the easiest ways of decorating plain paper. Here are methods for applying a design to tissue paper and for creating an interesting texture on thicker paper. Designs on soft tissue paper are best suited to wrapping delicate objects; use the sturdy, textured paper for heavier gifts. For more tips on cutting stencils and stenciling with paint, see page 143.*

STENCILING TISSUE PAPER

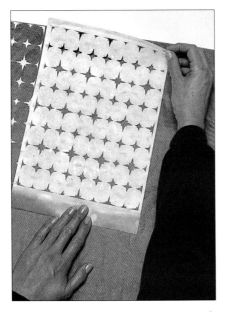

MATERIALS

Stencil sticks or paints
Stenciling brush
For the tissue paper:
Homemade stencil
(see pages 150-153)
Tissue paper
For the textured paper:
Strong brown wrapping paper
An iron
Two contrasting homemade stencils
(see pages 150-153)

1 Place stencil on the tissue paper and stipple paint through. Lift it up carefully and reposition, lining it up with the pattern you have already made.

2 Repeat until the paper is covered, then leave to dry for up to two days (depending upon the paint used) keeping the paper completely flat.

Opposite: You can stencil a design onto almost any paper, including tissue paper, crepe or even ordinary brown wrapping paper.

TEXTURING PAPER

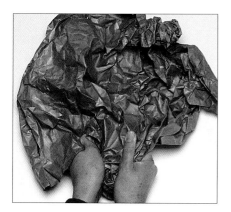

1 Scrunch the brown wrapping paper into a ball, pressing it firmly to crease it and break the sizing (protective coating) that covers the shiny side.

2 Flatten the paper with your hands and iron it on a low setting, shiny side down. Work outward from the middle to prevent it curling.

3 Place the first stencil in the top left corner of the paper and apply the paint. Continue until the paper is covered, then leave to dry.

4 Take the second stencil overlay and position it carefully on the paper, making sure that the two designs form a complementary pattern.

5 Then stipple through the stencil using a different color paint. Continue in this way until you have completely covered the paper, then leave to dry.

GIFT BOX

G *IFT BOXES are simple yet satisfying to make and will ensure your presents are noticed under the Christmas tree. You can scale the box up or down in size as necessary by increasing or reducing the template (see page 154) on a photocopier.*

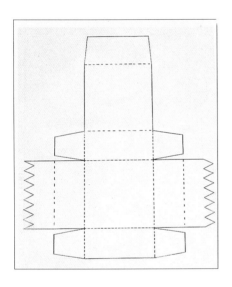

1 Using an HB pencil, trace the template on page 154 onto tracing paper. The dotted lines on the template indicate the position of the folds.

MATERIALS
4B pencil
Tracing paper
HB pencil
5 x 10 in. (12.5 x 25 cm) piece of card
Metal ruler
Scalpel
Cutting mat
Double-sided tape

2 Rub a soft 4B pencil over the traced lines, making sure that you cover both the box's outline and all the internal fold lines.

3 Turn the tracing paper over and lay it over the card. Using a ruler and the HB pencil, draw over the traced lines, pressing firmly.

4 Put the card on a cutting mat and, using a scalpel and metal ruler, cut around the outside, being particularly careful along the serrated edges.

Left: A contrasting ribbon and a gift tag made from a scrap of leftover card complete this stylish gift box.

5 Using the reverse side of the scalpel blade and the ruler again, lightly score along the dotted lines to make them easier to fold.

6 Place a piece of double-sided tape on each of the four flaps (marked with a cross on the template) and peel off the backing tape.

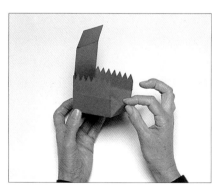

7 Fold up the flaps and press them against the sides of the box to fix them firmly in position. The box is now ready to use.

PAPER BASKET

A WOVEN BASKET *is the ideal container for small gifts such as homemade candies or for awkwardly shaped presents. When choosing paper for the basket, makes sure that it's colored on both sides, so the basket looks as good inside as it does outside.*

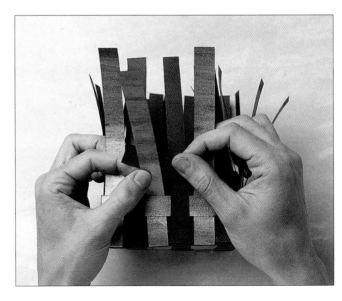

Opposite: A square basket woven from red and gold paper strips and filled with candies in matching wrappers.

1 Weave together 6 strips laid horizontally and 6 vertically to make a square central "mat", alternating the colored strips as shown. Glue the corners of the mat in place.

2 Fold up the free ends to make the sides and weave 2 more red and 2 more red-and-gold strips through to form the basket shape. Glue ends neatly in place.

3 Trim the untidy ends of the strips of paper and fold each one over and glue down. This will form a neat rim to the woven basket.

4 To make the handle, take the wider red-and-gold strip and make horizontal slits in it at 3/4 in. (2 cm) intervals. Weave the remaining narrow red strip through the slits, then glue the decorative handle to the basket.

MAKING A CARD AND ENVELOPE

U*SE THIS method to make up basic cards and envelopes, then decorate the cards using the suggestions on the following pages.*

MAKING THE CARDS

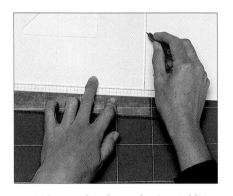

1 Using a ruler, draw a horizontal line twice the finished width of the card. Draw vertical lines for the edges and center fold.

2 Draw a horizontal line for the top edge of the card. Use a set square to get accurate corners.

3 Working on a cutting mat and using a ruler and scalpel, carefully cut around the outline of the card.

4 Lay the card right side down and score along the center fold with the back of the scalpel blade.

5 Rub out the pencil marks before folding the card along the center line. The card is now ready to decorate.

MAKING THE ENVELOPE

1 Adjust the template on page 155 to fit your card, then copy it onto tracing paper and rub a soft pencil over the traced lines.

2 Turn the tracing paper over and place it on the paper for the envelope. Use a ruler and an HB pencil to transfer the design to the paper.

3 Working on a cutting mat, carefully cut around the outline of the envelope, using a ruler and a scalpel for best results.

4 Use the blunt edge of the scalpel blade to score along the dotted lines, which indicate the side and top flaps. Rub out any pencil marks.

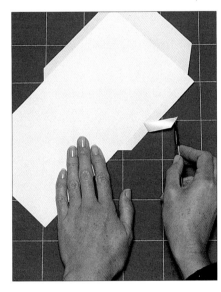

5 Turn the envelope over and place double-sided tape along the side flaps. Peel off the backing paper using the tip of the scalpel blade.

6 Turn the envelope over again and fold the side flaps in toward the center so that the double-sided tape is uppermost.

7 Fold up the envelope to form a pocket. Press down into the double-sided tape. When you come to seal the envelope, use glue or more tape.

CUTOUT
REINDEER CARDS

Y*OU CAN modify these cards by varying the number of reindeer. For a professional effect, take your time and fold the white paper very carefully before you cut out the reindeer.*

MATERIALS

Card
Thin white paper
Scissors
Pencil
Thick colored card
Spray mount
Scalpel
Sequins, glitter, etc., for decoration

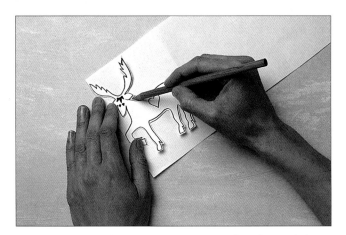

1 Copy the template on page 149 onto stiff card. Decide how many reindeer you want to cut out and fold the white paper accordingly, concertina-style, so that the template just fits onto the top face of the folded paper. Draw around the reindeer template.

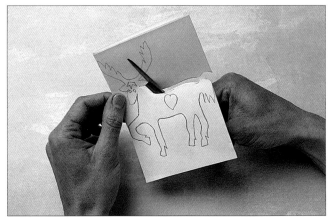

2 Cut out the reindeer but without cutting around the left-hand antler, raised foreleg and tail – the points at which the design is linked. Use a scalpel to cut out the hearts in the middle of the reindeer; if you do this neatly, they can then be used to decorate the card.

3 Cut to size the colored card that will form the greetings card and fold lengthways. Spray one side of the reindeer with spray mount, lay them on the colored card and smooth down gently.

4 Use glitter and sequins to embellish the card further, gluing them to the card with tiny dabs of clear glue. If you want to make your own envelope, follow the instructions on page 135.

VICTORIAN CARD

T<small>HE</small> V<small>ICTORIANS</small> *were fond of cards like these, that allowed the sender to write a special message under a lift-up flap. Today, such a card is bound to become a treasured keepsake.*

MATERIALS

Homemade stencils (see page 156)
Paper
Thin card
Green and red stencil paint
Stenciling brush
Cutting mat
Scalpel
Pencil
Double-sided tape

1 Lay the stencil for the border on a sheet of paper. Use the brush to stipple red paint onto everything except the holly leaves in the corners and leave to dry.

2 Wash the brush and then apply green paint to the holly leaves, first making sure that the stencil hasn't moved in the meantime. Leave the design to dry.

3 Cut around it with a scalpel. Stencil the holly motif from page 156 on to a piece of card the same size as the rectangle within the design.

4 Lay the card on the cutting mat face down and score a line slightly below one long edge using the blunt side of the scalpel.

5 Stick double-sided tape along the scored edge and use it to fix the stenciled card to the center of the rectangle to form the lift-up flap.

COLLAGE CARD

THIS FOUR-COLOR stenciled Christmas wreath of roses, holly, and ivy gains a three-dimensional effect from adding gold bows and red and green ribbon curls (instructions on page 141).

1 Mark the edges of the wreath by drawing two circles 3 and 6 in. (7.5 and 15 cm) in diameter on the tissue paper. Using the first overlay, stencil the rose hips and some roses in red.

2 Use the second overlay to apply pink paint to some of the remaining roses and then the third overlay to apply gold paint to the rest of the roses.

MATERIALS

White tissue paper
Four homemade overlaying stencils
(see page 157)
Red, pink, gold, and green stencil sticks
or paints
Stenciling brush
Ready-made glossy white card
All-purpose glue
4 gold ribbon bows
Red and green ribbon curls
(see page 141)

3 Using the fourth overlay, stencil the holly and ivy leaves in green. Then carefully cut out the stenciled motif, keeping close to the edge.

4 Stick the wreath onto a ready-made glossy white card, making sure you keep the tissue paper smooth. Glue on ribbon curls and gold bows.

TECHNIQUES

TYING A TWO-LOOPED BOW

1 Take a length of ribbon and tie it around a wrapped present. Hold one end in each hand.

2 Make a loop with one end of the ribbon and hold it tightly in one hand, close to the present.

3 Take the loose end and wind it around the first ribbon loop.

4 Feed the loose ribbon up between the first loop and the scetion you have just wound around it and pull tightly to form a second loop.

TYING A FOUR-LOOPED BOW

1 Take a long length of ribbon and tie it around the present. Hold one end in each hand.

2 As for a two-looped bow, make a small loop with one end of the ribbon and hold it firmly.

3 Make a two-looped bow as described above. Make the loops the same size, leaving long ends of ribbon.

4 Hold the long ends of ribbon at right angles to the first two loops.

5 Make a third loop with one of the free ends of ribbon and tie a second bow.

6 Adjust the loops to the same size, and check that they do not overlap. Trim off any excess ribbon, if necessary, to neaten.

MAKING RIBBON CURLS

1 Take a length of ribbon and cut along its length, stopping ½ in. (1 cm) short of the top.

2 Hold the uncut end and run the blade of a pair of scissors along one strand.

3 Repeat with the other strand. Pressing the blade firmly onto the ribbon makes it curl tightly.

4 If the curl looks too tight, pulling gently will help loosen it.

MAKING MOCK BOWS

1 Take a length of ribbon and mark the center near the lower edge. Decide how wide the finished bow should be, halve the measurement, and mark points "X", half the finished distance from the center, near the top edge.

3 Draw up the bow, pulling it into shape.

2 Bring a needle and thread from the back of the ribbon through the center. Fold the ends around and pass the needle through points X at the front.

4 Draw up the thread and bind the center of the bow tightly. Stitch the bow to hold it in place.

MAKING RIBBON ROSES

1 Take a length of ribbon and fold down one end diagonally.

2 Make a small inward-facing fold at the corner.

3 Roll the ribbon from the folded end, holding it in place with small stitches.

4 Fold the ribbon diagonally toward you.

5 Roll until the ribbon is straight and stitch again.

6 Repeat the process until the rose is the right size.

DRYING APPLE SLICES

  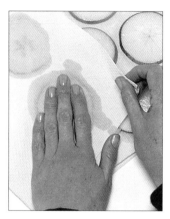 

1 Cut the unpeeled apples into slices around ¼ in (6 mm) thick.

2 Immerse the slices in heavily salted water for ten minutes to prevent them from discoloring.

3 Remove the apple slices from the salted water and gently pat them dry on kitchen paper.

4 Using a needle, thread the slices onto a length of cotton, tying a knot between each one to separate them. Hang to dry in a warm place for 3-4 days.

DRYING CITRUS PEEL

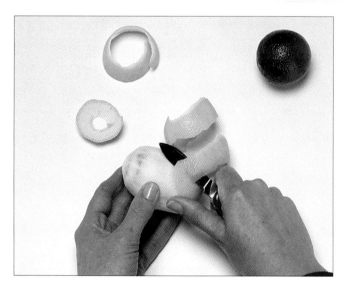 

1 Cut a spiral of orange or lemon peel. Use a sharp knife and try not to break the spiral if possible.

2 After 2-3 days in a warm, dry place, the peel will have dried to a hard, brittle finish and have developed a slight curl.

CUTTING STENCILS

1 Using a hard pencil, trace your chosen design onto tracing paper.

2 Rub a soft pencil over the traced lines, making sure not to leave any out.

3 Turn the tracing paper over and place it on your stencil material – card drawing film or acetate can be used. Trace over the design again with a hard pencil.

4 Place the stencil material on a cutting mat or a piece of thick card and carefully cut around the design with a sharp scalpel.

STENCILING IN COLOR

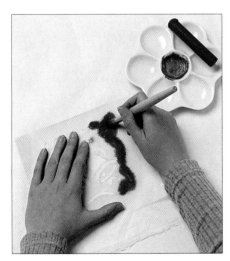

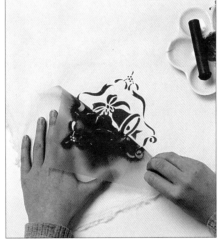

1 Position the cut-out stencil on your chosen paper and hold it firmly so that it cannot slip. Keeping the stencil brush almost upright, dab paint through the stencil.

2 Carefully peel back the stencil so that the paint does not smudge. Water-based paint dries rapidly, within minutes, but you may have to wait up to 48 hours for oil-based paint.

3 Almost any paper can be stenciled, from thick smooth card, to rough handmade paper and even thin tissue paper. For best results use a bristle brush to apply paint.

TEMPLATES

TRANSFERING THE TEMPLATES

To transfer any of the templates on these pages onto card or paper, use the following method:

- Trace the design onto tracing paper.
- Using a soft pencil, heavily draw over the lines on the reverse side of the tracing paper.
- Lay the tracing paper, right side up, onto the card or paper and draw over the design one more time. The pencil marks on the reverse of the paper will then be transferred to the card and paper ready for use.

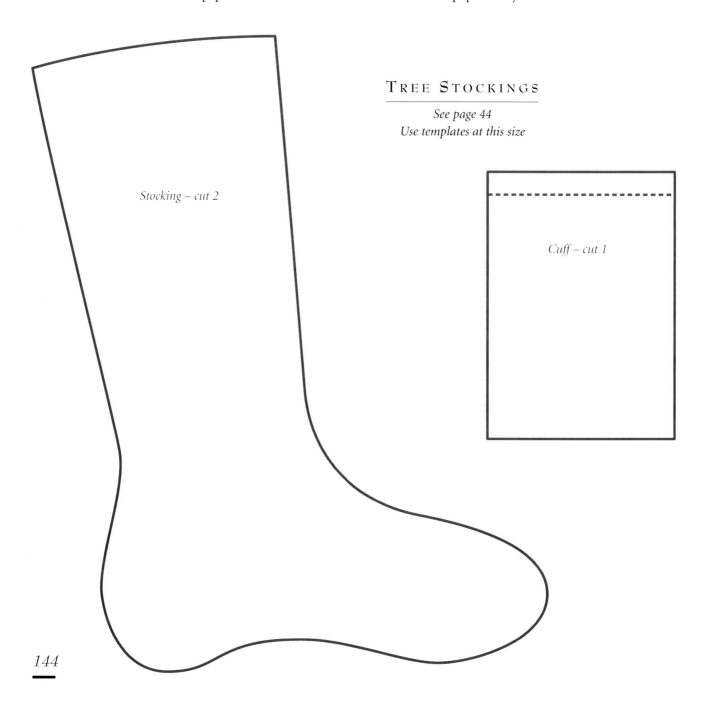

TREE STOCKINGS

See page 44
Use templates at this size

Stocking – cut 2

Cuff – cut 1

Section 1

ADVENT CALENDAR

See page 14
Use templates at this size

Section 2

Pot

Section 3

Section 4

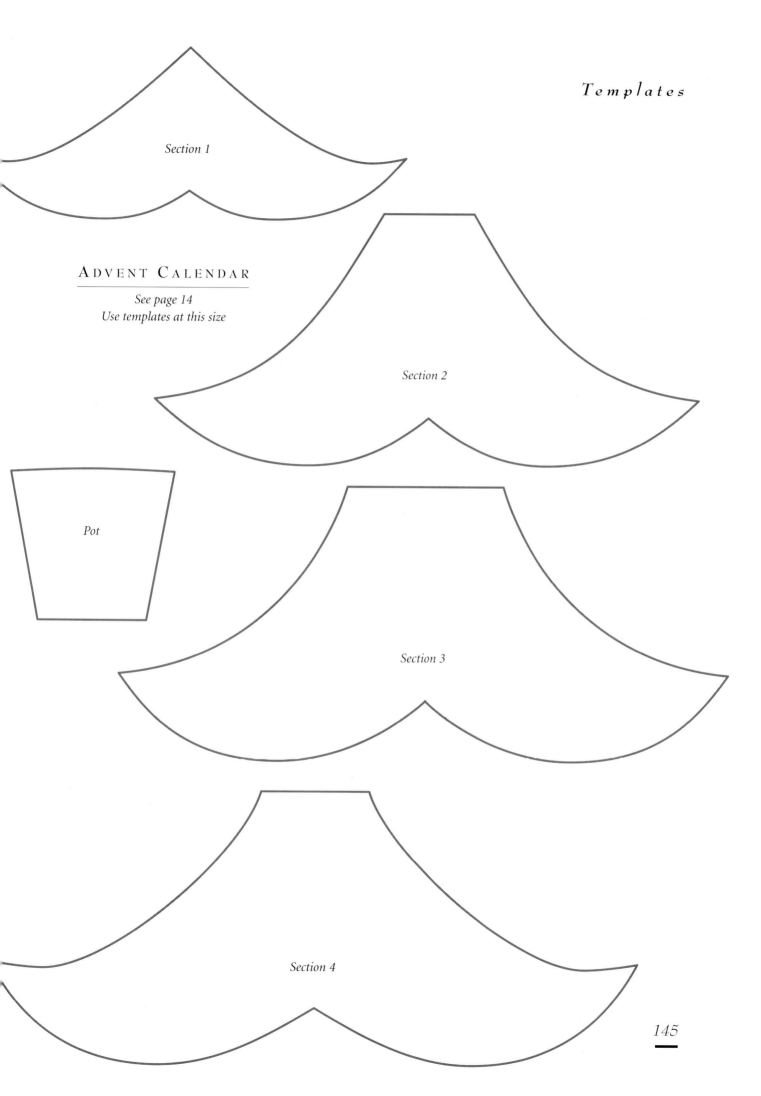

TOY SOLDIERS

See page 112
Use templates at this size

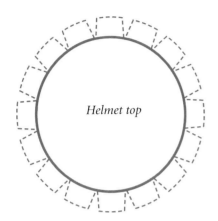

Helmet top

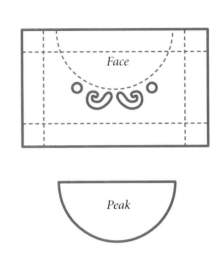

Face

Peak

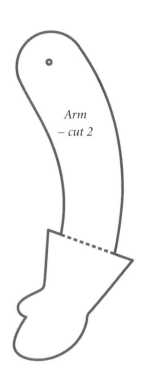

*Arm
– cut 2*

GINGERBREAD HOUSE

See page 88
Enlarge templates on a photocopier to 200%

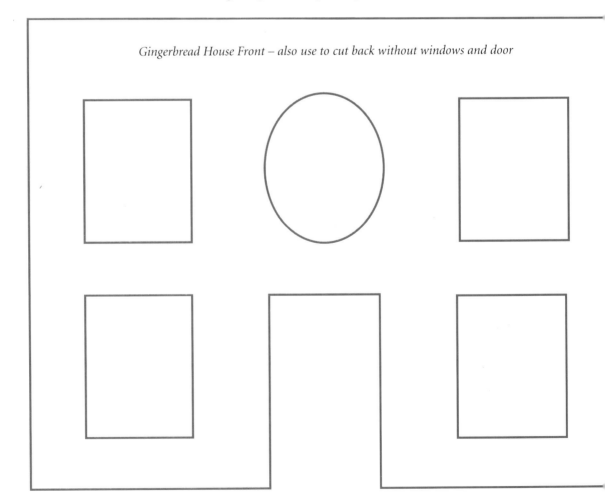

Gingerbread House Front – also use to cut back without windows and door

GINGERBREAD HOUSE

See page 88
Enlarge templates on a photocopier to 200%

Roof – cut 2

Side – cut 2

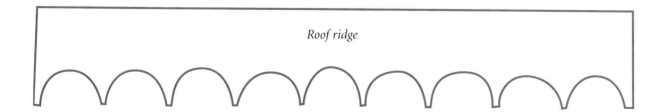

Roof ridge

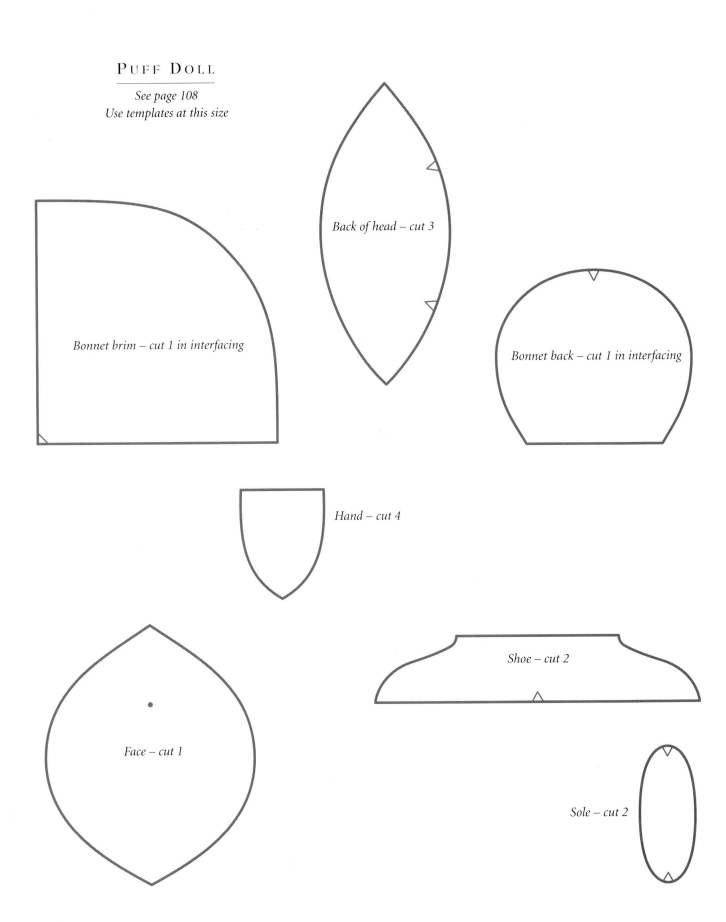

PUFF DOLL

See page 108
Use templates at this size

Bonnet brim – cut 1 in interfacing

Back of head – cut 3

Bonnet back – cut 1 in interfacing

Hand – cut 4

Shoe – cut 2

Face – cut 1

Sole – cut 2

PAPERCUT GARLANDS

See page 30
Use template at this size

LEAFY ALUMINUM GARLAND

See page 38
Use template at this size

REINDEER CUTOUT CARD

See page 136
Use template at this size

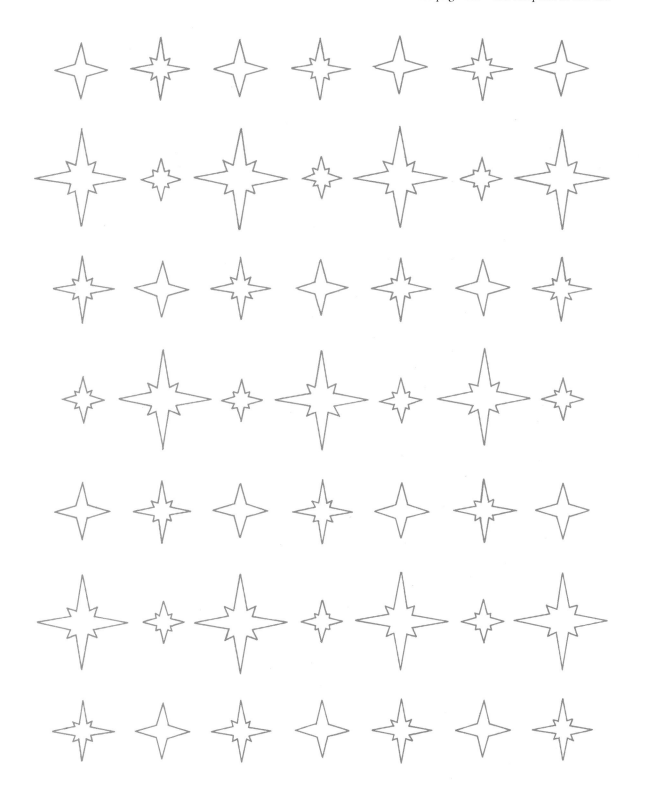

Stenciled Wrapping Paper

See page 128 – use template at this size

S TENCILED W RAPPING P APER

See page 128 – use template at this size

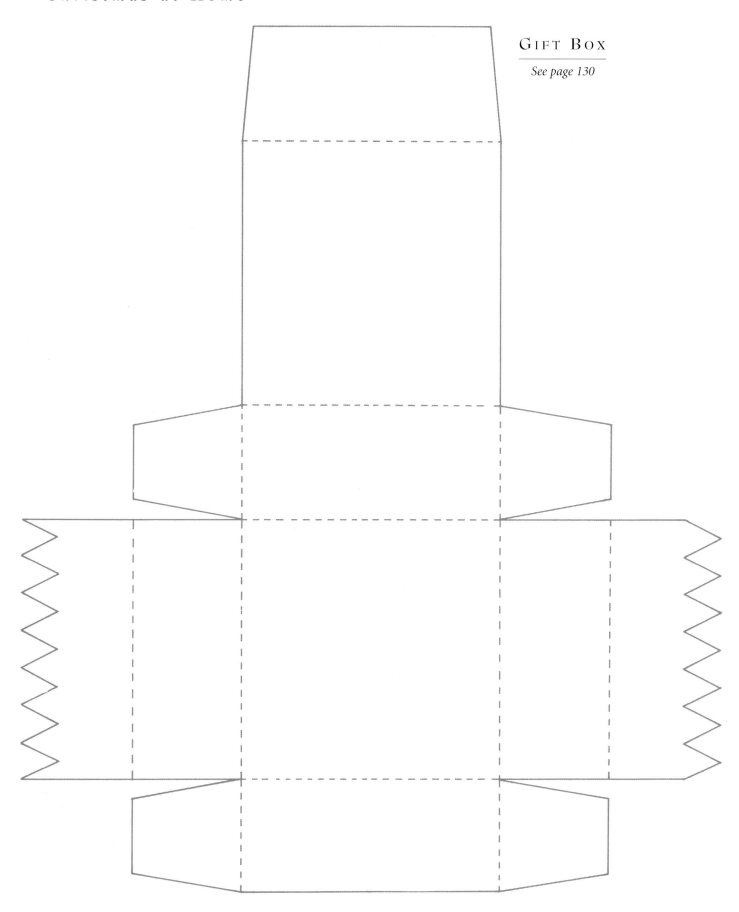

GIFT BOX

See page 130

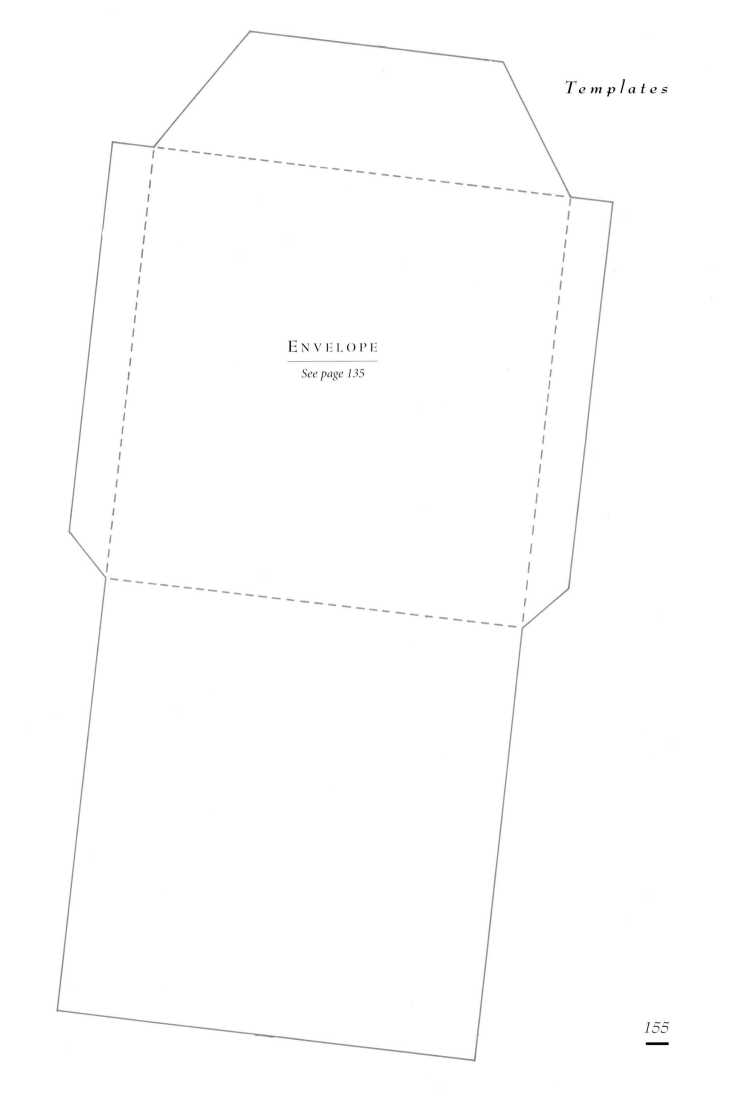

ENVELOPE

See page 135

INDEX

ACKNOWLEDGMENTS AND PICTURE CREDITS

Pages 7-13, 18-23, 26-29, 32-35, 44-49, 54-59, 62-75, 78-85, 128-131, 134-135, 138-140, 141 top, 142-143, 150-159 from *Christmas Crafts* by Carol McCleeve, photography by Matthew Ward, illustrations by David Ashby (Collins & Brown, 1995).
Pages 2, 24-25, 30-31, 38-39, 88-90, 124-127, 146 below, 147, 149 top right and left from *Traditional Christmas Crafts* by Deborah Schneebeli-Morrell, photography by Heini Schneebeli (Collins & Brown, 1997).
Pages 36-37, 60-61, 86-87, 91, 93, 95, 98, 101-105, 108-114, 118-121, 141 artwork from *Victorian Christmas* by Valerie Janitch, photography by Di Lewis, food photography by Patrick McLeavey, artwork by Coral Mula (Anaya, 1993).
Pages 1, 40-43, 96, 115-117 from *Beautiful Homemade Presents* by Juliet Bawden, photography by Jon Bouchier (Collins & Brown, 1998).
Pages 5, 50-53 from *Decorative Doughcraft* by Lynne Langfeld, photography by Shona Wood (Collins & Brown, 1996).
Pages 14-17, 76-77, 132-133, 136-137, projects made by Claire Worthington; pages 106-107, 122-123, projects made by Kate Haxell; style photography by Jacqui Hurst, step-by-step photography by Sampson Lloyd.
Pages 92, 94, 97, 99-100 photography by James Duncan.
Pages 144-145, 146 top, 148, 149 below, templates by Dominic Harris.
Jacket: front from *Christmas Crafts*; jacket back, left to right, top to bottom: project by Kate Haxell; from *Victorian Christmas*; from *Traditional Christmas Crafts*; from *Christmas Crafts*; project by Claire Worthington.